ADDING LIFE TO OUR YEARS

ADDING LIFE
TO OUR YEARS

by RABBI SIDNEY GREENBERG

with a foreword by RABBI MORRIS ADLER

JONATHAN DAVID/PUBLISHERS

New York

ADDING LIFE TO OUR YEARS
Copyright 1959, by Sidney Greenberg

Library of Congress Catalog Card No. 59-10539

PRINTED IN THE UNITED STATES OF AMERICA

TO

OUR DAUGHTERS' GRANDPARENTS

WHOSE LIVES ARE

SERMONS

CONTENTS

Foreword

The potential influence and significance of Jewish preaching in this country is eloquently suggested by two undeniable circumstances. The first is that no other Jewish endeavor reaches as many individuals in the course of a year, which makes preaching the largest educational effort carried on in American Jewish life. The second is that no other forum on the Jewish scene, addressing itself to large numbers, is capable of speaking out of as broad a perspective, as deep rootedness and as many-sided an involvement in Jewish matters as the pulpit.

It will be noted that I have referred to the "potential" rather than the actual influence of the pulpit. Unfortunately, a number of factors conspire to circumscribe its effectiveness and to limit the scope of its impact. There is the general devaluation of the word—written and spoken—which as one of the discourses in this volume points out, is a symptom of the moral confusion of our times. There is a not uncommon attitude which insinuates itself even into the view of a nominal adherent, which sees religion at its best as an irrelevance and at worst as an impediment. Such an evaluation does not stimulate serious attention to the religious interpretation. There is the smug contentment of a large segment of the religious community with an unexamined tradition, grimly indifferent to the adventure and sacredness of man's continuing quest for truth and knowledge which alienates those who might otherwise be respectful of religion's intentions. And there are all too many shallow preachers who, lacking a deep personal commitment, speak out of the extensiveness of their vocabulary or their well-stocked file, rather than out of the depth of their conviction and the compulsion of their faith. All of these tend to reduce the sermon to a formality, solemnly to be heard and then, disregarded.

Within the Jewish community another condition has tended to limit the influence of the sermon. The synagogue has for some time been relegated to the background by the tragic and compelling urgencies of Jewish need and sorrow in other lands. American Jewry has superbly mobilized itself in a vast enterprise devoted to the sacred tasks of rescue, relief and rehabilitation, and has placed this activity at the center of its concern. This large and bold effort has understandably loomed above the synagogue and its program as it brought to the fore a type of lay and professional leadership primarily, if not exclusively, devoted to its prosecution. The historic determination of American Jews to serve as their brother's keeper tended unintentionally to place the synagogue in the suburbs of communal attention and interest.

A movement is now evident, in a more than geographic sense, to suburbia. The recent renewal of interest in the synagogue is equated only by the over-optimistic with a religious revival. Yet it seems to me that it cannot be gainsaid that beneath all the sociological causes of the so-called return, there runs a stream of disillusionment with the conventional articles of faith that our expanding and self-assured national and economic life hitherto stimulated. There is abroad an unarticulated disquiet which economic well-being, political statesmanship, social reform and scientific advancement are not, singly or in unison, capable of alleviating. This uneasiness may lead to a greater hospitality to the fundamental insights and accumulated wisdom of our religious tradition. Never before in my lifetime did an opportunity of equal measure exist, of bringing before our people the tested truths of religious faith with the hope of an alert and attentive response. Needed are teachers of religion adequate to the opportunity. Such teachers will have to be at home in the spiritual tradition they represent, intimately conversant with the complexities and pressures of the modern world, deeply sympathetic with the dilemmas and anxieties of contemporary man, open-minded to the new knowledge gathered by research into human motivation and behavior and capable of applying with clarity and imagination the wisdom of the ages and of the age to present-day challenges.

Rabbi Sidney Greenberg is a gifted, sensitive and dedicated spiritual forth-teller. Judaism has in him an articulate and devoted interpreter who enlivens the tradition with knowledge of modern disciplines and adorns it with the felicity and charm of his own gracious personality. Preaching is for him a serious endeavor, worthy of a man's best. He expounds the great insights of the Jewish spirit with eloquence and reveals their relevance to our times with perception. He invokes modern thought and literature as well as ancient teaching and fuses them in a seamless unity of impressive instruction. He never scolds. Recognizing that anger has no place in the educational process, he does not descend to petulance or give way to irritability. Nor is he ever guilty of that ultimate sin of the preacher, self-righteousness. He includes himself in the congregation to which he directs his words. He challenges, he guides, he expounds and above all, he makes demands upon his auditor even as he does upon himself. His is a way not of convenience or of outer respectability, but of responsibility, discipline and dedication. His words are invariably inspirited not alone with a concern for values and principles but also with a humane and sensitive regard for the individual person. Hence he often deals with the personal difficulties and confusions of men imprisoned in the massive corporate, anonymous, standardized structure of our industrial society. Devoted to timeless truths, he is keenly aware that men must live and act out their destiny on the stage of the epoch and the world they live in.

That these spoken words which have deeply moved those who have heard them may in their written form reach and uplift a far larger congregation, is my earnest prayer.

RABBI MORRIS ADLER

xi

A Word to the Reader

One of the giants of the American pulpit, Phillips Brooks, once cautioned a class of theological students to beware of the day when they stood up in the pulpit without shaking knees. I confess that his advice was not wasted on me. Indeed, I followed it long before it came to my attention. In the sixteen years that I have been preaching, I have never approached the preparation of a sermon or its delivery without a potent dose of what our sages called, "emata d'tziburah—awe of the congregation." This quaking sense of apprehension is fearfully intensified as these sermons are released for publication.

Many a preacher maintains with ample justification that a sermon, unlike the proverbial child, should be heard and not seen. The sermon by its very nature is an intimate message conceived and delivered in a living context. The bonds of friendship and affection which link the rabbi to his people, the exalted mood of the Sabbath or Holy Day on which the words are spoken, the very atmosphere of the synagogue itself, all unite to enrich the message far beyond its intrinsic merit. The same message reduced to the cold and impersonal printed word, must now be prepared to forego the unearned advantages it initially enjoyed.

Stylistically, too, there are impressive differences between the spoken and written words. The speaker cannot afford the subtlety and the sophistication of the writer because he is aware that his listener must grasp his message at once. He cannot reread a passage. The preacher will therefore tend to be repetitious and obvious. Neither quality enhances the written word.

Notwithstanding these assorted misgivings, these sermons are appearing virtually as they were preached in response to a variety of weighty considerations. Chief among these have been the repeated requests of my congregants for written copies of sermons which had made a special impact upon them. In a very real sense these sermons are as much their property as mine. Their needs have served as my motivations. Their predicaments have been my texts. From the crucible of their experience I have distilled my themes. By their constant loyalty they have provided me with the utmost stimulation to search for answers commensurate with the earnestness of their questions. Thus they have been much more than passive listeners to these sermons. They have almost literally drawn them out of me. Their right to these sermons can therefore neither be contested nor denied. This book enables me to acknowledge their claim and to attempt to satisfy it.

There was another important consideration. In the commerce of ideas I have been an embarrassed debtor. As I have made abundantly clear in one of my sermons,[1] I have borrowed heavily for my ideas and my meagre store of knowledge from benefactors living and dead. It is far beyond my ability to discharge adequately so heavy an obligation but neither am I absolved from attempting some measure of repayment. This book represents a sincere effort to add my modest contribution to the flow of ideas and the interchange of cherished convictions.

My last, and by no means insignificant purpose, relates specifically to the Jewish scene. There are unmistakable signs that genuine religious impulses are astir in the heart of the American Jew. Every day brings mounting evidence that indifference is giving way to curiosity and curiosity is in many instances yielding to inquiry. The contemporary Jew is in a mood to learn more about himself and his heritage, his Jewish obligations and opportunities. He should, therefore, be exposed to as many voices as possible which summon him to his ancestral faith, which underscore its beauty and nobility, and which attempt to relate its message to his perils and perplexities, his hungers and his hopes. In this sacred task, every voice counts for something.

There remains now only the pleasant task of expressing my warmest gratitude first to my esteemed colleague, Dr. Morris Adler. He has been as kind in his deeds as he has been charitable in his words of praise. Through his lucid foreword and his many constructive criticisms, he has mightily enhanced the value of this volume.

---

[1] Cf.—"Humility—A Lost Virtue"

xiii

I am also most deeply appreciative of the cheerful and efficient assistance rendered by Mrs. Albert Wanicur, who typed virtually the entire manuscript and also struggled heroically and victoriously with my hieroglyphical script. Mrs. Thelma Simmons who typed a portion of the manuscript has also earned my genuine thanks.

My beloved wife and helpmate, Hilda, is part of these sermons in a most vital way. She attended their birth and agonized through their delivery. Her availability at all times as an audience of one contributed immeasurably to the refinement of the ideas in their developmental stages. The congregation, the reader and I are also deeply indebted to her for many a sermon I did not preach.

It is impossible to enumerate all who have left their abiding spiritual and intellectual imprint upon my thoughts and words. But neither can I refrain from singing out for grateful and reverent mention the name of my beloved teacher, Professor Mordecai M. Kaplan. His uncompromising insistence upon intellectual honesty and moral integrity in preaching, together with his repeated emphasis upon the sanctity of the spoken word, converted the task from a routine weekly obligation to a sacred and self-searching discipline. The magic of his personal zeal and earnestness transformed the study where the sermon is prepared and the pulpit where it is uttered into holy ground. Whatever merit this volume may contain is largely traceable to the benevolent impact of his influence.

Above all, I thank a gracious God whose extravagant generosity has far exceeded my humble desserts. Chief among my blessings has been the opportunity to serve in His vineyard where the labor is sweet and the rewards impressive. May this modest offering help bring the reader closer to Him and to His Torah. "May the words of my mouth and the meditation of my heart be acceptable unto Thee, O Lord, my Rock and my Redeemer."

SIDNEY GREENBERG

Temple Sinai
5 Tevet, 5719
January 15, 1959

ADDING LIFE TO OUR YEARS

ADDING LIFE TO OUR YEARS

One of the central preoccupations of science is with the problem of how to add years to man's life. Judaism is concerned with the problem of how to add life to our years. How can we deepen and enrich our years?

Preached on Yom Kippur, 1952

1

Adding Life to Our Years

O NE of the unquestionably great scientific achievements of the modern age has been the prolongation of the human life span. A brief glance at the comparative statistics of the life expectancy of men and women as it is today and as it was a mere half century ago is sufficient to drive home the happy truth that our life expectancy has been dramatically expanded in a remarkably short time.

But somehow, at Yizkor time, these statistics do not overly impress us. In our heart of hearts we feel life's brevity. How quickly the past year seems to have sped by! It does not feel like twelve months since last Yom Kippur. Indeed, all the years seem to be flying these days. Mothers under the canopy whisper, "It seems like only yesterday I was rocking her to sleep." A father after his son's graduation murmured to me recently: "I just couldn't believe it when I saw him claim his diploma. I was still thinking I'd have to lead him up by the hand." The years, like everything else nowadays, are travelling at accelerated speeds.

In many a heart too, there is a void left by the recent passing of a loved one. Last year we exchanged greetings. This year we're saying Yizkor. And many had so many unlived years! Statistics on the prolongation of human life offer little solace here.

If these personal reflections are not poignant enough we open our prayer book and a series of striking similes hammer home the awareness of life's brevity and transitoriness.

On each of the High Holy Days we repeat the passage which begins with the words: "Man's origin is the dust and his destination is the dust." And as for the interval between these two

1

climaxes the passage goes on to make quite vivid its fleetingness. "Man's life may be compared to a broken potsherd, a dried up blade of grass, a flower that fades, a shadow which passes, a cloud which evaporates, dust which floats and a dream which vanishes." Scarcely a slow motion picture of the human adventure!

The contrast is completed by setting our limited days against the eternity of God. "Thy years have no measure nor is there any end to the length of Thy days." Compared to the everlastingness of God, our lives are but a faint tick on the clock of eternity.

But if we pause to examine carefully those very similes which the Prayer Book uses to convey the sobering fact of life's brevity, I think we can find a significant difference between them and it is in this difference that I think we may also find an insight into the problem of handling life's brevity. If science is concerned with the problem of adding years to man's life, Judaism is concerned with adding life to man's years. And a clue to the kind of life Judaism would have us pour into our years may be found in a second unhurried look at the passage in the Prayer Book.

Let us take first the two phrases—"the shadow which passes" and "the flower that fades." To be sure they both suggest vividly life's brief duration. But as we examine them further we discover a profound difference between them.

What does the word "shadow" suggest to us? A shadow is something which has no independent existence. The form it has at a particular moment depends upon the shape of the object upon which the light is falling and upon the angle at which the light is striking the object. At 3 o'clock the shadow has one shape, at 5 o'clock another and when the light disappears, the shadow must likewise disappear. The expression "chasing shadows" has become in the English language a symbol of futility. For who can grasp that which has no substance, is merely a darkened reflection of something else?

How different is the picture which the word "flower" conveys. Oliver Wendell Holmes said: "The Amen of nature is always a flower." "Flowers," said Henry Ward Beecher, "are sent to do God's work in unrevealed paths and to diffuse influence by

2

channels that we hardly suspect." Wilberforce wrote, "Lovely flowers are similes of God's goodness." To Goethe flowers were "the beautiful hieroglyphics of nature with which she indicates how much she loves us."

Now, the shadow and the flower are both fleeting but it makes all the difference in the world whether we make of our lives flimsy shadows or beautiful flowers.

All of us know people who resemble one or the other. Many show no more independence of mind and thought than the formless shadow. Whatever thought they possess, whatever action they perform is merely a reflection of someone else's judgment, a response to someone else's urging. They take no trouble to form their own opinions or to plot their own course. There are many whose opinions reflect the last rumor they heard, their actions are an expression of the current rage. Pale, lifeless imitators, they possess neither color of their own, nor direction, nor purpose.

This, incidentally, is what dictatorship, whether of the right or left, tries to do to its subjects. It tries to strip them of their individuality, rob them of their ability to think for themselves. They must be guilty of no independent thinking. The dictator or the party will do the thinking, they will reflect the party line. Deviation is not to be tolerated. Hence the goose-stepping, the slogan chanting, the lavish parades, the thought control.

The sad part is, that what dictatorship imposes, some free people deliberately choose. Unwilling to pursue the discipline of study and thought which alone can produce independence of mind, they pick up the contemporary slogans and prejudices and become part of the anonymous mob. The extent of their contribution to society can be only too well imagined.

Then, of course, there are those who, like the lovely flower, possess their own uniqueness and individuality, who enrich the landscape of which they are a part; those, who by their own goodness and gentleness, "do God's work in unrevealed paths" and make it easy for us to believe in the basic goodness of all men.

That is the kind of influence many of those whom we remember this day had upon us. Many of us are fortunate enough

3

to be able to remember a father or a mother or a brother or a mate of whom we could say as did Matthew Arnold of his father, who was a teacher, the headmaster of Rugby. . . .

> "And through thee I believe
> In the noble and great who are gone,
> Pure souls honor'd and blest
> By former ages, who else . . .
> Seemed but a dream of the heart,
> Seemed but a cry of desire.
> Yes! I believe that there lived
> Others like thee in the past . . .
> . . . souls tempered with fire
> Fervent, heroic and good
> Helpers and friends of mankind."

"Small souls," it has been finely said, "help the world by what they do, great souls, by what they are." They are the living flowers in the human garden.

Yes, the shadow passes and the flower fades but it makes all the difference in the world whether we make of our lives flimsy, formless shadows or beautiful, lovely flowers.

Let us contrast further two other similes in the passage: "dust that flies," . . . "a dream that vanishes." Again, they both convey the sense of life's brevity but at this point the similarity ends. For the contrast between dust and dreams is literally as great as between earth and heaven.

What are the qualities of dust? Dust is an irritant. If it gets into the eyes or invades the nose or throat it brings distress and discomfort.

Unfortunately, many lives are like dust which flies. They possess a unique capacity for irritating people. There are some people who have the unhappy faculty of bringing out the worst within us. They may be the ones who are always criticizing you for your own good, never suspecting for a moment that an occasional compliment may also be for your good. They never weary of rehearsing their own good fortune in such a way as to excite your envy rather than your joy. They are people whose train of thought is utterly without any terminal facilities and when they have an hour to kill usually decide to spend it with someone who hasn't. After they are gone they usually leave us muttering with exasperation: "I don't know why but he always rubs me the wrong way. He always gets my dander up." Some people bring happiness wherever they go. These people bring happiness whenever they go. They irritate and distress.

Dust has another unattractive characteristic. When it is not flying about doing its irritating work it has a tendency to settle and it settles on the lowest level it can find.

How many of us do just that—settle on the lowest level we can find? Especially in our choice of leisure activities is the tendency to settle on the lowest possible level exceedingly strong. It seems that just as there is a physical law of gravity which pulls an object down so is there a social law of gravity which tends to pull us humans down. And we have to be especially careful against this downward drag. If you want to test your own resistance to this social tendency ask yourself a series of questions.

If you have a choice between a pulp novel and a serious book, which do you choose?

If you have a choice between a regular Tuesday night game and a Tuesday night study group which do you choose?

If you have a choice between conversation and gossip, between a television program and a Friday Night Service, between making and a Tuesday night study group, which do you choose?

In contrast to dust which irritates and sinks there is the dream which inspires, which elevates, which points to new horizons, which opens up new frontiers.

The motto which Theodore Herzl chose for his novel was: "If you will it, it is no legend." And he closed with this warning: "But if you do not will it, then it remains a legend which I have recited. Dreams and action are not as widely separated as many believe. All acts of men were dreams at first and become dreams again."

Every worthwhile human achievement, if traced back far

enough, began as a dream. Youth Aliyah began as a dream in the heart of Henrietta Szold.

A reborn Israel began as a dream in the heart of the prophet Isaiah.

The freedom we enjoy began as a dream in the heart of a slave people in Egypt.

The medicines which heal us, the discoveries which sustain us, each began as an uplifting, inspiring dream.

There are many whose whole lives "are such stuff as dreams are made on." They bring upliftment, they evoke the very best within us, they challenge us to new achievement, they unfold before us new hope, new possibility, new opportunity. In his autobiography, "As I Remember Him," Hans Zinser speaks of his father "whose love enclosed me while he lived and whose hand I have felt caressingly on my head throughout my life whenever I was in need of comforting."

Yes, the dust floats away and the dream vanishes, but it makes all the difference in the world whether we make our lives like dust, irritating and sinking or like dreams soothing and uplifting.

Thus we can re-read that whole passage in the Prayer Book and see actually a series of alternatives. We can make our lives like the potsherd with its jagged edges, which is an obstacle on the human pathway, or like grass which clothes the earth, feeds the animal and, thus, sustains man. We can make our lives like the cloud which blots out the sun or like the caressing wind that softly brings relief.

Yes, life is brief, but we determine its quality. Indeed, precisely because it is brief we must be very discriminating as to what we put into it. We are like the man leaving on a journey with a small leather pouch. Shall he fill it with mud when he can take along diamonds? Shall we fill our days with pettiness and greed when close at hand are kindness and generosity? Shall we degrade or uplift, discourage or inspire, stagnate or grow?

We can not determine what the New Year will bring to us but we have the more important choice—what we bring to the New

Year. Shadows or flowers, dust or dream, what shall we make of our lives?

George Bernard Shaw's declaration might well serve as a watch-word for the New Year: "Life is no brief candle for me. It is a sort of splendid torch which I have got hold of for a moment and I want to make it burn as brightly as possible before handing it on to future generations."

DOORS

Doors are constantly being closed on us in life. This is an inescapable truth. But it need not depress us or defeat us if we bear in mind one of God's merciful compensations.

Preached on Yom Kippur, 1957

2

Doors

DEATH, the poets tell us, has a thousand doors. Sometimes it closes a door slowly on the creaking hinges of drawn-out illness so that we have time to steel ourselves for the grim inevitability that awaits us. At other times, death springs a trap-door which slams in our faces with terrifying and stunning suddenness. But whether death heralds its arrival or catches us unawares, one thing is certain. It bolts tight a door to a precious life and leaves us with a sense of loneliness, yearning and aching emptiness.

When we stop to consider the matter further, we realize that it is not only death which closes doors on us. Life does that very thing—less dramatically, less conspicuously, perhaps, but no less emphatically.

Shakespeare in his oft quoted passage in "As You Like It," divides life into seven ages. Man begins as "the infant mewling and puking," and then, he is "the whining school-boy, with his satchel and shining morning face, creeping like snail unwilling to school." Later he is the lover "sighing like a furnace"; then the soldier "seeking the bubble reputation even in the cannon's mouth." In his 5th age he is "the justice in fair round belly with good capon lined." In his 6th age we find him "with spectacles on nose and pouch on side." Shakespeare brings this procession to an inglorious conclusion by ending with "second childishness," when we find our hero "sans teeth, sans eyes, sans taste, sans everything."

Now we may not agree with Shakespeare's division of life. Students of human behavior today are more inclined to trace the growth of personality in emotional stages—infancy, childhood, adolescence and maturity. But whatever the categories we use, Shakespeare was eminently sound in telling us that every stage of life is separated from the next by "exits and entrances," by the closing of doors.

The pretty little girl leaving hesitantly for her first day in the nursery school has closed a big door of life behind her. The 9 year old en route to his first overnight camp, waving a reluctant good bye to his parents from the bus as he fights back the tears, has closed a big door of life behind him. The quaking Bar Mitzvah boy standing alone before a congregation chanting prayers and making pledges, has closed a big door of life behind him. The prim little 12 year old, acting like 15 as she glides out with her first movie date, has closed a big door of life behind her. The hopeful young man who has just "popped the question" has, at the same time, closed a big door of life behind him. And when years later he proudly negotiates that three mile walk down the fifty foot aisle with his daughter leaning ever so gracefully on his arm, he knows what every parent knows after the marriage of a child, that he has closed a big door of life behind him.

All of life is a constant succession of closing doors each accompanied by its own internal revolutions and peals of alarm.

This is true not only of our emotional life but also where our physical capacities are concerned. Here, too, the doors sometimes swing shut violently accompanied by a resounding crash. There is an accident or a heart-attack and we awake to find that a whole series of hitherto automatic and almost effortless actions are now out of bounds. Small, "normal" exertions, feeding oneself, shaving oneself, walking a few steps—actions so small and so normal that we were scarcely aware of them, much less, experienced gratitude for being able to perform them, now become infinitely precious because a door has been slammed between us and them.

Most of the time, however, life is closing doors behind us very softly, so softly we scarcely hear the lock snap. And then one day we awake to the realization that we can no longer spend fourteen hours a day at the office, that perhaps we had better start heading for the club-house after the 9th hole, that maybe the Mrs.

has the right idea in suggesting a split-level home with fewer steps. We're not quite sure precisely when our physical capacity began to wane, when the distance between holes started to grow longer and the steps in the home steeper. We can't recall turning the knob on the door. Perhaps it was one of those new-fangled electronic doors which operates so sneakily and so noiselessly. But in our heart of hearts there is oppressing certainty that a door of life has been closed quite securely.

Yes, life, no less than death, is a constant series of doors being closed.

Having made these none-too-cheerful observations, I think that we are now ready for our first important truth about this matter. It is this: A vital index of our maturity as men and women is the gracefulness with which we accept the closing of the doors, which death and life alike impose. That such acceptance is often enormously difficult goes without saying. But unless we prove capable of doing precisely that, we forfeit the opportunity to live creative and meaningful lives.

When death closes the door to a life we have loved it is worse than futile to spend the rest of our days in vain efforts to batter down the door, or in asking the unanswerable question, "Why did the door have to swing shut on me?"—or, in pretending that the door was never closed at all.

I am thinking of a very unhappy woman who, for years after her husband's death, has not permitted one item of his clothing to be removed or one piece of furniture in his study to be rearranged. "I want things to be just as they were when Bill was here," is her explanation. She may be soothing herself with the thought that she is being loyal to his memory but that poor woman is betraying her future. Unfortunately, she has not yet come to terms with the reality that the door on her Bill's life has been shut tight.

As human beings, in our quest for maturity, we often have a strong hankering to retrace our steps down life's corridor and re-open the doors of infancy and childhood. Then, life was protected and sheltered; then, all our needs were catered to, all life centered around us, all decisions were made for us. Small wonder then that when life becomes complicated and perplexing we should want to run back, to rewind the spool of time.

Psychologists call this phenomenon "regression." The married woman who is forever solving her marital problems by packing off for mother's, the harassed head of the family who meets every financial crisis by getting another asthma attack so that the burden of worry is shifted to other shoulders—each of these has failed to accept graciously the inescapable fact that the doors of infancy and childhood have been sealed tight. They can beat on the doors of the nursery and dress in the faded wardrobe of childhood but only at the cost of remaining emotional dwarfs with overgrown bodies. Growing up, if it has any meaning at all, means that we avoid the hazardous and unrewarding effort to pick the locks on the doors that have closed on our yesterdays.

And what shall we say of those who refuse to pay the toll on the bridge of time by pretending that they are still as young as their kind friends tell them they look? What the doctor said of Jim is true of many Americans, I am afraid. When Jim collapsed in his office the examining doctor who had known him well confided to a mutual friend: "Jim sacrificed for his beliefs." "What beliefs did he cherish?" the friend asked. "Jim believed," answered the doctor, "that he could live a 30 year old life with a 55 year old body."

Many of us harbor such suicidal beliefs. Too often, as our powers wane, our ambitions flourish. When we should be diminishing our financial pressures we are building them up; when we should be curtailing our social round we are expanding it; when we should be pumping the brake, our foot finds the accelerator. We pay a heavy penalty indeed when we refuse to accept gracefully the inescapable fact that life has closed some important doors in our physical lives quite securely. We cannot break these doors. We can only break ourselves against them.

We are now ready to proceed to our second truth—one suggested by a brief but beautiful prayer found in the N'eilah service on Yom Kippur. "Open to us a gate at the time when a gate is closed." The author of the prayer was underscoring one of the basic truths of the spiritual life.

God never closes a door in our lives without at the same time opening another. Whenever one area of life is sealed off to us, another comes into view.

I had a vivid illustration of this truth while working on this very theme. I was writing in my study at home and had closed my door. Suddenly a gust of wind blew through the adjoining bedroom and slammed shut the bedroom door which had been open. But the impact of the door that slammed forced open the door to my study. This is what happens in life all the time.

The implications of this truth are profound indeed. They touch upon every aspect of life and death. Our tradition sublimely insists that death itself is the closing of one door and the simultaneous opening of another. "This world," taught our sages, "is only a vestibule before the palace of the world to come." When the door closes on the vestibule, it opens into the palace. There are a host of compelling reasons which nurture our faith in the immortality of the human soul. The reasonableness of the universe demands it for, as the physicist Robert Millikan said: "The Divine Architect of the Universe has not built a stairway that leads to nowhere." Our own souls hunger for it and God has given us no hunger which He does not satisfy. We hunger for food and He provides food. We thirst for drink and He provides water. We hunger for love and He has put love into the world. We hunger for eternal life and I believe He satisfies that craving too. These are only some of the persuasive arguments which convince me of the truth that: "Death is not the master of the house. He is only the porter at the king's lodge, appointed to open the gate and let the King's guests enter into the realm of eternal day."

Yes, God does open to us a door at the time when he closes the door of death.

And how about us the living? What doors open to us when the door of sorrow closes?

The more I observe life, the more impressed do I become

13

with the large number of doors which open to us at such a time.

Do you remember the parable of the Dubno Maggid? He tells of a king who once owned a large, beautiful pure diamond of which he was justly proud for it had no equal anywhere. One day, through a mishap, the diamond sustained a deep scratch. The king called in the most skilled diamond cutters and offered to reimburse them handsomely if they could remove the imperfection from his treasured jewel. But none could repair the blemish. After some time a gifted lapidary came to the king and promised to make the rare diamond even more beautiful than it had been before the accident. The king was impressed by his confidence and entrusted his precious stone to his care. And the man kept his word. With superb artistry he engraved a lovely rosebud around the imperfection and he used the scratch to form the stem.

A deep truth speaks to us out of this parable. When sorrow inflicts a bruise upon us, we can use even the scratch to make our lives more radiant and more lovely. Sorrows are often "the needles with which God sews our souls to eternal truths."

Despite its grim appearance, sorrow possesses vast potential power to expand our horizons, to deepen our understanding, to enlarge our visions. It has played a transforming role in the lives of countless bereaved who could say in a mood of melancholy gratefulness with Wordsworth: "A deep distress hath humanized my soul."

Through the door of sorrow we can enter into the suffering of others. Our human compassion is kindled. Our sympathies are awakened. It can elicit from us powers of fortitude and patience which, but for it, might never have been quickened into life. Sorrow can also help purge us of pettiness and selfishness. It can, thus, bring us closer to our fellow man and help make us taller people. God does, indeed, open to us a door at the time when He closes the door of sorrow.

As we grow and develop, God is forever opening doors in front of us as He closes doors behind us. Our mistake is that we lose heart, we don't trust Him. We know where we've been but we don't know where we are going. We want things to be just as they were in "the good ole days." To have faith in God, means among other things, to believe that the door He now opens to us leads to a stage of life with its own unique satisfactions and delights, its own rich adventures and challenges. As our physical powers diminish added time and energy become available for life's less taxing but no less rewarding activities. We have more time to study, to reflect, to listen to music, to cultivate friendships, to help along a cause, to elevate our souls, to get to know ourselves better.

Life would become drab indeed and quite insipid to our taste if the years of our lives were not kissed each with its own charms and capacities, each with its unique colors and shadings. Life's beauty comes precisely from the changing configurations and patterns of the years, from God's great mercy in constantly closing and opening doors for us.

For last I have left two striking illustrations of our theme which deal not with the doors that are softly closed behind us but with the doors that seem to be maliciously slammed in our faces.

The first is a page from recent Jewish history. If ever there was a period of closing doors in Jewish life, it was in the holocaust of Nazi Europe. Indeed it was a horrible succession of N'eilahs for six million of our brethren—fathers, mothers and children. When we think of those dark, dreary, maddening years, we visualize the closing of the doors of crematoria, gas-chambers, railways cars, concentration camps. All exits were sealed off, every escape hatch swung shut. The allegedly civilized world did distressingly little to open the doors of doom. The British, then in control of Palestine, were busy hunting down and turning back the ships that managed to bring a few pitiful remnants of the disaster.

And yet it was precisely at this time, under the impact of the doors being slammed in the faces of our European brothers that the doors to Eretz Yisrael were forced open. Locks that had remained bolted for nineteen centuries were now sprung open and a new magnificent chapter began in the saga of Israel. God opened for us a gate at the time of the closing of the gate.

The second illustration points up this truth in the life of a single individual.

On May 3, 1941, Peter Putnam not yet 21 and a Junior student at Princeton University, with everything to live with and apparently nothing to live for, made an important decision. He was going to commit suicide. Carefully he wrote out his suicide note and stuffed it into his wallet. From his pocket he drew a gun loaded with three bullets. The hands on his purple leather travelling clock showed twenty past ten. It was the last thing Peter Putnam was ever to see. For it was at that moment that Peter Punam pulled the trigger of the gun pointed at his brain. Peter Putnam with the door of hope and zest for living seemingly shut in his face had taken the only way out.

Peter Putnam did not die but he had succeeded in blinding himself for life. Surely we would imagine if Peter Putnam had felt no reason for living before his suicide attempt, he would feel even less reason for doing so now. Let us listen to him tell the story from this point.

"What surprised and exhilarated me, as I returned to consciousness, was not so much that I was alive, but that I was so terribly glad to be alive. . . . The future, including future blindness, seemed a challenge to which I was now wholly committed, and this challenge transformed my view of the world. Graduation from Princeton, a meaningless formality toward which I had been stumbling with half a heart, now seemed the very symbol of my first step toward this new world. In short I wanted to live as I had never wanted to live before."

In February 1942, accompanied by his seeing eye dog Minnie, Peter was back at Princeton. He helped write and direct the Princeton Triangle show and acted in it. He graduated Magna Cum Laude, and went on to earn his Masters and Doctors degrees. In the meanwhile he found time to get married, to raise a family of three children, to learn how to ski! He now teaches and writes. His second book, "Cast Off the Darkness," has just appeared.

Peter Putnam in his darkness saw the door God opened for him after all the doors had been shut tight.

I said earlier that what we pray for is that God should open for us a gate at the time when a gate is being closed. I'd like to emend that somewhat now because you see we don't have to ask God to do that for us. God is always doing precisely that. What we should pray for is that we be granted the courage and the patience to find the door He opens at the time when doors close; that we do not despair, that we do not surrender our faith and our hope, that we hold on tenaciously until we find the way to renewed life and renewed zeal.

Two stanzas from "Opportunity," by Walter Malone, can serve as a fitting closing to our theme because they call attention to life's unending possibilities.

> "They do me wrong who say I come no more,
> When once I knock and fail to find you in.
> For every day I stand outside your door,
> And bid you wake and rise and fight to win.
>
> Weep not for precious chances passed away,
> Weep not for golden ages on the wane.
> Each night I burn the records of the day,
> At sunrise every soul is born again."

MAKING MOUNTAINS OUT OF MOMENTS

There are mountains in time no less than in space. One of our basic needs is to experience the uplift of great moments periodically. A tried and tested method of answering this need is readily at hand.

Appeared in "Best Jewish Sermons of 5713"
Preached on Rosh Hashanah, 1952

3

Making Mountains Out of Moments

IT is very instructive to note that some of the most crucial events in the spiritual unfolding of our faith took place on mountains.

In this morning's Torah reading, Abraham's willingness to serve God at the ultimate price, the sacrifice of his son, is tested on the mountain—Mount Moriah. The central religious drama in Israel's history, the revelation of the Torah, takes place on the mountain—Mount Sinai. When Moses before his death is afforded a glimpse from afar of his Promised Land which to his heartbreak he may not enter, he is standing on the mountain— Mount Nebo. When the zealous prophet Elijah calls his people to make a final and fateful choice between serving God and worshipping idols, he is standing on the mountain—Mount Carmel.

It is not difficult to surmise why mountains should have been chosen as the site for these significant occurrences. Goethe correctly observed: "On every mountain-height is rest." On the mountain we find the serenity and quiet usually denied us on life's Main Street. Withdrawn from the deafening clamor of life's obligations and burdens, we are in a better position to think and to meditate.

Dr. Ferdinand C. Lane in the foreword to his sensitive book, "The Story of Mountains," underscores the penetrating psychological insight of the psalmist when he exclaimed: "I will lift up mine eyes unto the mountains." He observes that the very act of lifting the face upward precipitates certain uplifting emotions which serve to elevate the soul of man above the sordid plane of the commonplace and to release it for wider horizons. "Up," he says, "has a thousand meanings to connote the desirable; 'down,' as many in the opposite direction. Happiness is always linked with the ascending scale; misery with the reverse. God Himself is known as the Most High."

Moreover, the mountain-top gives us a better perspective upon the country-side. We see more. We see further. We see better. We see the whole forest as well as the individual trees. We see things in clearer relationship to each other. "Whoever has not ascended mountains," said William Howitt, "knows little of the beauties of nature." And observing the multi-colored quilt of nature from on high we are somehow given the perspective to see life steadily and to see it whole, to better understand our place in God's scheme of things, our relationship to our fellow man and to the Maker of mountains Himself.

Now just as there are mountains in space there are mountains in time. Just as there are high places so are there high moments. There are certain crucial moments in life when we are suddenly uplifted, when our vision becomes clearer and our perspective better; moments when life's haze suddenly lifts and there is revealed to us a glimpse of beauty or an insight into truth we had never possessed. We can, and do, make mountains out of moments.

Many of us recall Keats' famous sonnet in which he describes his excitement when, for the first time, he read Chapman's translation of Homer: "Then felt I like some watcher of the skies when a new planet swims into his ken." Keats made a mountain of vision out of that moment of beauty.

One of the most stirring poems to come out of World War II was one found on the body of an unknown American soldier. He was obviously not a finished student or poet but he revealed a sincerity which was eloquent. Let me read a few stanzas:

> "Look God I have never spoken to you
> But now I want to say 'How do you do?'
> You see, they told me You didn't exist.
> And, like a fool, I believed all this.

20

Last night from a shell hole, I saw your sky
I figured right then, they had told me a lie . . .
Funny I had to come to this hellish place
Before I had time to see your face."

And a few stanzas later he concludes:

"Well I have to go now, God, goodbye.
Strange, since I met you, I'm not afraid to die."

Our anonymous G. I. made a mountain of faith out of his moment of peril.

From my own war-time experience I recall one dreary day in an army hospital corridor. A pilot who had crashed was on the critical list. His father and I were "sweating him out." During these interminable hours of the vigil, the father spoke from time to time: "If only my boy will live," he sobbed, "I'll ask for nothing more. I don't care if he's crippled or incapacitated. I'll take care of him. I'll sacrifice anything for him." And after a thoughtful pause: "You know, Chaplain, only yesterday I was complaining about the gasoline shortage, business difficulties, and all the things I suppose other people complain about. But how trivial, almost foolish, all these things are now." Yes only yesterday that father had been permitting a thousand petty irritations to grow into an ulcer—that wound-stripe of American civilization. But now, through his tears, he could see more clearly what really mattered for he had made a mountain of insight out of his moment of agony.

This, dear friends, is a common experience. In moments of great peril, severe illness or even bereavement we are often lifted up. Our vision is suddenly improved, our perspective adjusted and certain truths which we had only half sensed become bold beacons of light. Trivialities, whose importance we had exaggerated, are reduced to their proper size. The important things we had underestimated now become precious beyond words. Paradoxically, moments of darkness sometimes illuminate life's landscape. Perhaps this is what our sages meant when they said: "Some

21

acquire an understanding of the world about them in a single hour," if, we may add, they have the wisdom to make a mountain of vision out of a moment of trial.

But must we wait for crisis or danger or bereavement to give us insight? Is there no way of making mountains out of moments without first passing through the valley of the shadow?

For us who have gathered in the synagogue today the affirmative answer is obvious. In our personal lives it frequently takes a moment of traumatic, shocking character to give us insight. But in our collective lives as Jews we have available these sacred days, great mountain-peaks of the human spirit, from which we can obtain a sharper view of our lives. From the heights afforded by the collective wisdom and experience of Israel's poets and prophets, psalmists and sages, and distilled through our prayer book, we obtain a proper perspective upon life, upon our destiny in it and our relationship to one another.

From the peaks of these exalted moments we see many things that normally escape our view in the valley of daily living. Our irritations do not irritate quite so much, our worries appear transient because they are no greater than the ones that disturbed us last year and which, for the most part, never came to pass. The reasons for our quarrels with mates, family, and one-time friends appear insignificant because they like ourselves are bent under their personal pekel tzoros—their own human burdens. Our problems appear more soluble. Even our pain and heartbreak become more endurable when we see not a piece of life's puzzle but the whole design. We understand that in the divine scheme of things, without pain there could be no love, without tears there could be no joy, without darkness there could be no light. These are some of the things we see more clearly from the mountain peaks of these days.

And then, as Jews, there are certain things we see more clearly from the mountain of these exalted moments. We see that Jewish life is beautiful and it is great to be a Jew. "How fortunate are we, how goodly is our heritage." It is good to be home in the synagogue. It is good to associate once more with the Jewish

22

heroes of the past, our fellow Jews of today, and the Jewish ideals of peace, justice and brotherhood which are timeless. It is stirring to hear again the familiar melodies of the prayers—the plaintive *hineni*, the exalted Kaddish, the awe-inspiring *unesaneh tokef*. It is exciting to feel within the indefinable *pintale yid*, that latent, inextinguishable spark of Jewishness respond to the call of the tradition as it peals forth from the *Shofar*. It is humanizing to feel the finest within us, our highest aspirations, our noblest resolves, our most generous impulses—so often denied or disregarded in the valley of daily toil and strife—to feel all this come to the forefront of our hearts and minds. Yes, as Jews on this day we see what Edmond Fleg saw. In his youth, he renounced Judaism only to embrace it again ever more fervently in later life, after a period of intense study. In his book entitled "Why I am a Jew" he wrote:

"I am a Jew because born of Israel and having lost it I felt it revive within me more alive than I am myself.

I am a Jew because the faith of Israel demands no abdication of my mind. . . .

I am a Jew because in all places where there are tears and suffering the Jew weeps.

I am a Jew because in every age when the cry of despair is heard the Jew hopes.

I am a Jew because the message of Israel is the most ancient and the most modern."

Yes, these are some of the things we Jews see from the uplifting peaks of these days. And perhaps the more thoughtful among us will see something else too. Perhaps we will see that it is a terrible, terrible waste to descend from the mountains after these days are gone and not to climb up again until an entire precious year of our lives will have fled beyond recall. The psalmist in a probing question asked: "Who shall ascend the mountain of the Lord?"—and he went on to add: "And who shall stand in His holy place?" Many ascend the mountain, take a quick look around and, like summer vacationists, do not hope to return to the mountain until the following year at the same time. "Who

23

shall stand in His holy place?" Who shall regularly ascend the mountain of inspiration, the tall cliffs of clear perspective?

In our temple very many have not been content with a seasonal ascent. They have returned regularly to fill our synagogue, Sabbath after Sabbath, to stand on the mountain of *Shabbat* joy and peace.

During the past year our adult study group read very carefully Dr. Abraham Heschel's highly inspirational work, "The Sabbath —Its Meaning for Modern Man." In this poetic little book the author etches in unforgettable imagery the unparalleled greatness of the Sabbath and its tremendous potential contribution toward making our days on earth meaningful and radiant. "The Sabbath," he says, is "a day for being with ourselves, a day of armistice in the economic struggle with our fellowmen and the forces of nature." It marks "the exodus from tension." It is a day when we are bidden to banish personal anxiety, care and anger. "It is a day of harmony and peace, peace between man and man, peace within man and peace with all things. The Seventh Day," Dr. Heschel reminds us, "is a mine where spirit's precious metal can be found with which to construct the palace in time, a dimension in which the human is at home with the divine, a dimension in which man aspires to approach the likeness of the divine. It is not an interlude but the climax of living."

Achad Ha'am was absolutely correct when he said: "More than the Jew has kept the Sabbath, the Sabbath has kept the Jew."

Because I believe with all my heart that the Sabbath can be for each of us a powerfully uplifting peak, I appeal to you now to pledge yourselves to ascend that peak as often as possible. Last Rosh Hashanah we inaugurated this appeal. The response was excellent. Very many pledged and honored their pledge. For them, no further appeal is necessary to persuade them to renew their pledge. Their own satisfying memories will induce them to pledge to attend if possible even more frequently than last year.

To those who did not join in the weekly services with us and to the newcomers to our family I address my most urgent appeal. At your seat there is a Sabbath Attendance Pledge Card committing you to attend a minimum of once a month, or twice a month or every week. There is a separate pledge card for each member of the family. While we like to see families coming as a unit because we believe that "a family that prays together stays together," nevertheless we realize that it is often impossible for both husband and wife to attend together. At such times we do not want the inability of both to attend to become the excuse for neither to attend. We therefore ask husbands and wives to pledge separately—each according to his or her own circumstances and will. The will is most important for given the will to attend most of us can so shape our circumstances. We always have time for those things which really matter to us.

As you turn down the corner of your pledge cards remember that the act is a commitment to make mountains of inspiration out of Israel's sacred moments. Let each of us hear the Divine summons spoken to Moses:

"Come up to Me on the mountain and be there."

WHAT DO YOU SEE?

"Two men looked out through prison bars. One saw mud and the other stars." What we see in life depends largely on who does the looking. What do you see?

Preached on Rosh Hashanah, 1954

4

What Do You See?

THE biblical incident which figures most prominently in the Rosh Hashanah service is the story of the *akeda*, the binding of Isaac. We read it as our Torah portion on the second morning, we blow the Shofar which recalls the ram which was destined to take Isaac's place on the altar and we encounter a host of references to this towering episode throughout the liturgy of this day.

For our text this morning I should like to take a suggestive rabbinic comment with which our sages embellished the narrative. They tell us that as Abraham and Isaac and their servants approached Mount Moriah, the divinely designated summit for the sacrifice, Abraham turned to his servants with a question: "Do you see anything in the distance?" They stared and shook their heads. "No, we see only the trackless wastes of the wilderness." Abraham then turned to Isaac with the very same question. "Yes," said the son, "I see a mountain, majestic and beautiful, and a cloud of glory hovers above it." It was at this point that Abraham directed his servants to remain behind while he and Isaac continued on their mission alone.

Here then is our text for this day. Two people facing in the same direction, surveying the identical scene, come up with completely different impressions. One sees only emptiness and barrenness ahead. The second sees the majestic and challenging mountains. The difference obviously lay in the eyes of the beholder.

Skipping the centuries now and coming right here into the synagogue, let us each ask ourselves the question—"What do you see?" As we shall soon realize, this can be a decisive question.

Before we proceed to try to answer it, may I say that, in

many vital areas of our lives, a great number of us not only do not see anything but we scarcely seem to be looking at all. I often wonder during these days how many of us have fully grasped the thought that with the manufacture of the hydrogen bomb during the past year it is now possible for the human race to commit collective suicide. Nuclear scientists today quote an entry made in a scientific journal eighty-five years ago. At that time leading scientists predicted that within one hundred years "man would know of what the atom is constituted. When this time comes," the journal said, "God with His white beard will come down to earth swinging a bunch of keys and will say to humanity, the way they say at five o'clock at the saloon: 'Closing time, Gentlemen!' " We live at what might become closing time.

We see, therefore, how terribly much is at stake in the issues of peace and war, and yet so many of us are living behind our personal iron curtains through which these crucial questions never seem to penetrate.

Recently one of our national monthly magazines carried a two page spread boldly captioned: "The Big News from Paris." This was directly after the United Nations Assembly had completed a crucial meeting in the French capital. Mankind's nervous hopes had been focused on those deliberations. The headline in the magazine, therefore, compelled attention. Well, what do you think was being trumpeted as "the big news from Paris?" As you read on, you learned that "necklines will be lower, skirts somewhat longer and three new perfumes have been created. . . ." To too many Americans, this is not only the big news, it is the only important news. Crucial days and trivial interests! People for whom life's decisive issues are resolved in the arena of fashion.

Lest I be accused of being a little severe with some of the ladies, may I hasten to add that I am not unappreciative of sartorial grace, nor do I minimize the high morale value of a new hat. What I am saying is that when these things loom too large on our personal horizons, we simply do not see the things that matter. And this is true whether we are preoccupied solely by fashion, or sports, or the card tables, or any other form of recreation. As a matter of fact, the same is true if we permit the business of making a living to become all consuming. If we are hypnotized by any of these matters, the vital matters go by default. Willy Loman's wife put the thing simply in "The Death of a Salesman": "Attention must be paid."

Unless we pay attention to the things that matter most, whom shall we blame if demagogues make off with our civil liberties, if our teen-agers become, not a source of hope but a source of danger; if Judaism becomes for us an unknown quantity and its majestic voice is reduced to an inaudible whisper; if the home becomes—as someone cynically remarked—a place to pick up the car keys; if the State of Israel becomes victimized by a hostile State Department policy?

"Where are you looking?" is, therefore, an important preliminary question.

Now, while it is possible for us to avoid looking at certain issues, however crucial they are, there is one thing we cannot avoid facing—life itself. On this day when we pray for life, we might, therefore, each ask ourselves—*what do you see in life?* Let me break this large question down to three smaller questions.

When you look at your life, do you habitually see reasons for grumbling or gratefulness? Do you feel that you have been shortchanged or over-paid? Do you constantly feel your cup is half empty or in the words of the psalmist, "my cup runneth over?"

Matthew Arnold has written that "one thing only has been lent to youth and age in common—it is discontent." Our favorite posture is one of protest and we who have so much, so very, very much, often permit the one thing we lack to blind us to the great wealth we possess.

Whenever I am on the verge of indulging in the unearned luxury of feeling sorry for myself, I recall something the late Rabbi Milton Steinberg said to his congregation in a sermon which was later printed. He told them of the first time he got out of bed after a long illness and was permitted to step out of doors.

As I crossed the threshold, sunlight greeted me. This is

my experience—all there is to it. And yet, so long as I live, I shall never forget that moment.

The sky overhead was very blue, very clear and very, very high.

A faint wind blew from off the western plains, cool and yet somehow tinged with warmth—like a dry chilled wine. Everywhere in the firmament above me, in the great vault between earth and sky, on the pavements, the buildings— the golden glow of the sunlight. It touched me, too, with friendship, with warmth, with blessing. And as I basked in its glory there ran through my mind those wonder words of the prophet about the sun which someday shall rise with healing on its wings.

In that instant I looked about me to see whether anyone else showed on his face the joy I felt. But no, there they walked, men and women and children, in the glory of a golden flood, and so far as I could detect, there was none to give it heed. And then I remembered how often I too had been indifferent to sunlight, how often, preoccupied with petty and sometimes mean concerns, I had disregarded it. And I said to myself—how precious is the sunlight but, alas, how careless of it are men. How precious—how careless! This has been a refrain sounding in me ever since.

It rang in my spirit when I entered my own home again after months of absence, when I heard from a nearby room the excited voices of my children at play; when I looked once more on the dear faces of some of my friends; when I was able for the first time to speak again from my pulpit in the name of our faith and tradition, to join in worship of the God who gives us so much of which we are so careless.

Milton Steinberg discovers the sunshine after a heart attack and the psalmist realizes that his cup runneth over after he walks through the valley of the shadow.

What do you see? The bleak wilderness of discontent or the beautiful mountain of thankfulness?

May I ask another question now?

When you look at life, do you see only your life and your needs, or do you see the lives and the needs of others as well? Do you see life as a campaign of acquisition or as an adventure in sharing? This question is basic because it spills over into every area of life. How do you regard your job or profession? Is it only a means of providing you and your family with your needs and luxuries, or is it also an opportunity to render a service? How do you regard your mate in marriage? Someone created for your comfort and convenience or someone whose life you can enrich and ennoble? How do you regard your fellow-man? Someone whose main function in life is to serve as a stepping-stone to your success or someone with hopes and needs just like yourself?

In "The High and the Mighty," there is one line spoken very quickly which is especially worth remembering. On the dramatic plane trip, Mr. Joseph is telling the passenger across the aisle how his well-laid plans for a dream trip to Honolulu kept going awry at every point. Nothing seemed to go right. Like the time they came to the hotel at which they had made advance reservations only to find that their room had been given by mistake to another Mr. and Mrs. Joseph from Ogden, Utah. And Mr. Joseph says: "Well, I figured maybe they had had a dream too."

Do you look upon your fellow man as someone who maybe has had a dream too; who has children who worship him as much as yours do you; who wants his little place in the sun as desperately as you want yours, who hungers for that word of encouragement and appreciation as much as you do; who, in brief, is a man created like yourself in the image of God?

I read recently about a little fellow who didn't mean to be impolite to his teacher, but, when he was asked to draw a circle and found himself without a compass and couldn't remember the name of it, he asked: "Miss Jones, may I take your circumference?" Well, I suppose some of us may be a little sensitive about our physical circumference, but that young fellow stumbled upon a vital question. What is your circumference? How large is

31

the area of your concern, whom and what do you include in the circle of your vital interests?

Do you feel, for example, that what happens to Israel is your personal concern? Does its security and economic stability worry you at all, or do you feel that having purchased a bond some time ago and having once belonged to the Zionist organization, you have completely and forever discharged your obligations in that direction?

One of the most moving books I ever read is a thick Hebrew anthology called "G'velay Esh—Scrolls of Fire." It contains the writings of the boys and girls who fell in Israel's war of liberation. Their pictures in the back of the book remind one of a college year book. One piece there is entitled, "At Your Grave My Brother Ephraim." It was written by Zvi Guber, who entered the Haganah at sixteen and gave his age as seventeen so that he could join.

The eloquent tribute to his fallen brother Ephraim concludes with these words: "My brother, I vow to you: 'My heart will be the candle of your soul and I shall cherish your memory within me like a precious treasure.

'In the very path where you met your death, I shall go, even though it be filled with pain and anguish, even though I knew for certain it is my last road.

'By the holiness of the pain and by the holiness of my love for you I swear this; by the holiness of all that makes life worth living and death worthwhile.' "

Three months later, Zvi was killed in action and was buried near Ephraim. Not far from their grave a new settlement has been built and named "The Village of the Brothers."

What do you see in life? An arid wilderness of selfishness or a challenging mountain of service?

We come now to the last and perhaps most decisive question. When you look at life, do you look with fear or with faith?

It is impossible, of course, to be entirely free of fear. There is literally no one without his share of fears and apprehensions. The bravest of men have a fear of losing loved ones, a fear of losing health and fortune. To a certain extent, of course, our fears are the saving of us. The man who fears failure develops his skills and his talents more fully. The fear of separation from loved ones spurs us on in medical and scientific research and "the beginning of wisdom," the psalmist tells us, "is fear of the Lord." But fear becomes a matter of deep concern when it becomes exaggerated and morbid, when instead of leading to action it creates a paralysis of will, when it succumbs to the very object of its dread.

In a children's book there is the fable of the oriental monarch who met Pestilence going to Bagdad. "What are you going to do there?" "I am going to kill 5000."

On the way back, the monarch met Pestilence again. "You liar," thundered the monarch, "you killed 25,000." "Oh, no," said Pestilence, "I killed 5,000. It was fear that killed the rest."

Beginning with the month of *Elul* and continuing through *Hoshana Rabba*, we add Psalm 27 to our daily Service. That Psalm might well be our watchword not only for these days but throughout the year.

"The Lord is my light and my salvation, whom shall I fear? The Lord is the fortress of my life of whom shall I be afraid?"

The cardinal irreverence in Judaism is to be afraid of life, for when we fear life we betray a lack of faith in God. Faith in God does not mean to believe that sorrow will never invade our homes, or illness never strike us and our loved ones. Many people who cherish such a naive belief are due for heart-breaking disillusionment. It is these people who will say to you: "When my mother died, I stopped believing in God." They believed the wrong things about God to begin with. To believe in God is to have faith that He will give us, amidst all vicissitudes, the strength to endure, and the power to hold on and see it through, the capacity to translate even our trials and our tribulations into moral and spiritual victories.

What do you see in life—the parched desert of fear or the inspiring mountain of faith?

33

May I conclude with a very brief parable which will sum up our theme and perhaps help us to remember it.

Two men went out one night to explore the world. One equipped himself with a lighted torch while the other went into the darkness without any light. When the second returned he said: "Wherever I went I found nothing but darkness." But the first one said, "Everywhere I went, I found light."

May God kindle in our hearts the torch of gratitude, the candle of service and the lamp of faith, so that wherever we go during the year ahead we may see light. Amen.

ON BORROWED TIME

When death strikes we must leave many tasks undone. How can we outwit death?

Preached on Yom Kippur, 1942

5

On Borrowed Time

O N Rosh Hashanah, our thoughts are focused upon life. At this moment before the Yizkor service, they are pre-occupied with the contemplation of death.

Death has ever perplexed us. Our rabbis go into great detail in describing the state of confusion on the part of Adam and Eve when their son Abel was slain. The stricken parents, we are told, were bewildered, not knowing what to do with the body until a raven came with its dead, dug a pit and laid the little raven in it. Adam and Eve then followed this example.

Their grief and perplexity an eminent sculptor tried to portray by carving in marble the story of the first death. In the strong arms of the father lies the limp form of the lifeless lad while the startled mother views the tragedy with conflicting emotions—melancholy, curiosity, anguish and despair.

The years that have passed since the first recorded death have not appreciably diminished the bewilderment and ignorance which surround that most unavoidable human phenomenon—death. The known world has radically changed during the ages. It has progressively marched forward conquering fields hitherto deemed uncontrollable. Man with seemingly limitless creative genius has wrested from nature its most cherished secrets. But one secret nature has kept to itself—the secret of death. This mystery remains bleakly before us, startling us with its suddenness and impenetrability. We still stand aghast and frightened before it even as did Adam and Eve. And especially before the memorial services of this day, we search for the key to the riddle. We ask ourselves: Is there nothing beyond life but death, and nothing beyond death but decay?

Hand in hand with the uncertainty as to the nature of death and as a revolt against the shortness of life, man has always felt a strong yearning for everlastingness, for immortality. Man has always expressed a longing for an endless eternity in which his body or his soul or both combined would continue to exist in some form or another above the ravages of time. I say "man," not only "the Jew," because the belief in some sort of a here-after is not limited to the Jewish religion. It is a common denominator in virtually all religions. The Egyptian mummies that have been discovered were often buried with food which they were expected to eat in the new world to which they passed. The Jewish conception was not quite so materialistic. Its *Gan Aiden* was more spiritualized. From man's earliest endeavors to find meaning in life, he has tried in different ways to prove immortality because he could not suppress his most urgent desire to believe it. Without it, human life was much too short. It was utterly meaningless and futile. Actually he could never prove immortality, but he believed it none-the-less. He believed it not because he could prove it, but he, forever, tried to prove it because he believed it. It seems a voice within him spoke that colossal word: "Man thou shalt never die."

This hunger for immortality is not limited to believers. Even men in the business world have been known to spend great sums in order to live on if only in name. P. T. Barnum, a hard-boiled gentleman if there ever was one, was greatly disappointed because he had no sons to carry on his name. He therefore offered his grandson C. H. Seeley $25,000 if he would call himself Barnum Seeley. Not very long ago, rich men used to pay authors to dedicate their books to them. They wanted immortality on a book cover. Libraries and museums owe their richest collections to men who cannot bear to think that their names might perish from the memory of the race. The New York Library has its Astor and Lenox collections. The Metropolitan Museum perpetuates the names of Benjamin Altman and J. P. Morgan.

We ourselves, in some cases almost in spite of ourselves, find that we do believe in some kind of immortality, or else we should not show so much respect for the departed. Do we merely cherish the memory of someone past who was and is no more? I hardly think so. We revere our departed ones because an inner voice whispers to us that all is not extinguishcd in death. It is this belief which confers a sacred character upon the deceased.

It is also this belief in immortality which has ever given meaning and purpose to life. It made heroes out of cowards and supplied mankind with its greatest sons and daughters. It enabled the Greek philosopher Socrates to accept death for the sake of the truth and to die, saying to his students: "And now we part, you to life and I to death, but which one of us to a better state, God alone knows." The belief in immortality armed Rabbi Akiba with the courage to die for the sake of Judaism exclaiming with his last breath: "Hear O Israel the Lord our God the Lord is One."

And so it is for these reasons—first, because man could not help believing in immortality and second, because it endowed life with purpose, that Judaism has always subscribed to a belief in deathlessness of the human soul. But, and this is important, Judaism has been strong in its insistence that immortality must be earned. It is a reward for righteous living. It is an achievement more than an endowment. "The righteous even in death are considered alive. The wicked even in life are considered dead."

Later in the day we shall read one of the most stirring epics in any literature—a description of the violent deaths suffered by ten of Israel's noblest sons at the hands of brutal Rome during the persecutions of the second century of the common era. One of the teachers, Rabbi Hanina Ben Teradion by name, was burned to death with a Sefer Torah wrapped around him. And there is a moving legend in our Midrash which says that while he was perishing in the flames, his eyes became aglow with a wondrous vision. His pupils noting the remarkable phenomenon, asked him: "*Rebbe, mah atta roeh?—*Our Master what do you see?" And he answered: "*Gvilin nisrafin v'oteyot porchot—*I see the parchment of the Torah being burned but the letters of the scroll are flying in mid-air." They are not being destroyed. The flames cannot reach the teachings of our Torah. The words live on. They are stronger than the flames.

In the fate of the martyr's scroll we hear intimations of his own divinely appointed destiny. He too will elude the flames. They will have to be content with meager fuel—his body. His essence is imperishable, and beyond the leaping tongues of fire. In the destiny of the martyr we hear intimations of our own deathlessness. Death can only claim our "parchment." Our "letters" are beyond its reach. The good that we do defies death.

Ah! But there is the rub. It is exactly at this point that the sting of death is hardest to bear. Death often comes before we can finish the writing on the parchment, before we can complete the work which we undertake. Death in itself may perhaps conceal many a hidden blessing for the human race beneath its grim mask. Those of us who are familiar with the theme of the play, "On Borrowed Time," will more readily agree to this. In that play, death is represented in the form of a man. One day, when he comes to pay "a call," the would-be victim succeeds in capturing death and he ties him up in a tree. As long as he is there he can claim no more people. Then the entire play is devoted to the struggle in the intended victim's mind whether or not he should release death. At the end, this perfectly intelligent and humane man releases death although he knows he will be the first victim, because his friend convinces him that this world of ours would be a very sad place to live in if the hopelessly crippled and the helplessly insane could never be freed from their misery. How unprogressive would humanity become if it became burdened with old age. Even ambitious youth would lose its ambition if it knew that it was not living on borrowed time, but that its days were limitless. It would become unproductive if it did not have the realization of life's brevity to spur it on to action.

Many a keen observer of life has extolled the role of death. Job, in his misery, spoke with heavy wisdom when he described the grave as a place where "the wicked cease from troubling and the weary are at rest." The Greek tragic poet Aeschylus went further when he wrote: "Men hate death unjustly; it is the greatest defense against their many ills." Nicholas Rowe, the English poet and dramatist of the eighteenth century paid death more than a reluctant tribute in "The Fair Penitent":

> Death is the privilege of human nature,
> And life without it were not worth our taking.
> Thither the poor, the pris'ner and the mourner
> Fly for relief, and lay their burthens down.

A rabbinic sage expressed a similar sentiment in commenting upon the verse in Genesis. "And the Lord saw all that He had made and behold it was "tov m'od—very good." "Tov m'od zeh hamavet—'very good' refers to death." A multitude of voices, thus, have been raised in defense of death in the divine scheme of things.

What makes death so unbearable however is that it often strikes us with our goals unachieved, our parchment largely still unwritten, our hopes unfulfilled, our dreams unrealized. Perhaps like the grandmother in "On Borrowed Time," we are sorry to go because we still have our knitting to finish; or like the grandfather we have the little grandson "Puds" to watch over. The sting of death is its untimeliness. When it calls we find that we must leave unfinished symphonies.

It is, therefore, against that aspect of death that we must protect ourselves. We must make sure that there are those who will carry on our work and complete our tasks after we are gone. We can do so in two ways. First, by identifying ourselves with worthwhile institutions and ideals. Emerson once said that an institution is the lengthened shadow of a man and there are many of us here today who see in this synagogue the lengthened shadows of their departed parents. Their parents helped to build this house of God, to organize it and to equip it. Their work lives on in this structure as a fitting tribute to their memories. While they themselves have not completed the task, they did lay the foundation, they erected the framework. Because their purpose was

41

noble, God has provided worthy successors to them who are carrying on that work. Yes, a man's deeds when they are rightly dedicated, survive him and serve to kindle the flame of his memory in the fireplace of posterity.

The second important investment we must make, if our life's work is to be completed, is in our children. A rabbi one day startled his pupils by saying: "Our father Jacob did not die." Whereupon, his pupils asked in understandable amazement, "Is the biblical account which tells of the death and burial of Jacob untrue?" "No," said the sage, "I did not mean to refute the physical death of Jacob. What I meant is *"Mah zaro bichayim af hu bichayim.—*Since his children live, he too lives." They are carrying on his traditions, they are trying to achieve his goals. They are his immortality.

We, who will soon recapture the sainted memories of our parents, cannot help but feel that though our departed parents are physically removed from us, they continue to pulsate in our hearts. The valuable lessons they taught us, the kindly advice they gave us, the ideals they implanted within us, all serve to make them always alive in our own lives. But let us remember that it is not enough to live on in our children only in name. We must live on in their work.

We will recall how sad Abraham was in his old age before Isaac was born. Now, Abraham had another heir, Ishmael; but Abraham knew that Ishmael might inherit his money but never his ideals. Abraham wanted a spiritual heir. If our life's work is to be completed when our hands have dropped the torch, we must educate our children to cherish what we hold sacred.

We, who are interested in the survival of Judaism, must help transmit that concern to our children. They must be taught to love its ideals, to share its faith and fulfill its hopes. History has willed that America has become the Jewish center of the world. The war has uprooted the European centers and shifted the center of spiritual gravity to these shores. American Israel will determine if and how Judaism is to survive. The responsibility placed upon our shoulders is a massive one. We dare not consider it lightly. So many of us while maintaining our own allegiance to Judaism are not effectively transmitting it to our children. And to the extent that we fail to do so, we are contributing to the disintegration of our religion.

The Talmud, in speaking about the laws concerning the extinguishing of a candle on the Sabbath, says: "If one extinguishes the candle on the Sabbath because he fears the thieves,"—he is afraid lest they see him and kill him—"then he has not violated the law." "But if he puts out the candle because he doesn't want to use up the wax or the oil, then he is guilty." How well may we apply this law today. In Europe, the lamps of Jewish learning have been put out. The *Cheder* and the *Yeshiva* in Poland, Russia and Germany are no more. But our Jewish brethren in Europe are free from blame—their study lamps were extinguished because of the thieves and the vandals. But when we, who enjoy religious freedom, permit the lamps of Jewish learning to be extinguished we are guilty because we do it because we want to spare the candle, we want to spare the oil and the wick. We have the means and the opportunity but we are not putting them to use.

What a sad irony it is that what thousands of years of frightful persecution could not rob from us, we are now giving freely away. Judaism which survived exile from Palestine, oppression by Babylon, captivity by Rome and the inquisition in Spain is being threatened by its own children in free America. Are our children going to carry on our life's work for us? We are living on borrowed time, but it is in our children that God gives us a second chance.

Thus, if we would rob death of its sting, we must not only lead dedicated and creative lives ourselves, but we must also provide those who will bear our torches and keep them glowing when our strength has failed. On this day of memorial let the memories we invoke inspire us to educate our youth to continue the heritage that we will bequeath to them even as we feel obliged to continue the heritage that our parents have bequeathed to us. Only then will we not be afraid of death because we shall have won our immortality and we shall become deathless, timeless, living on in others. Amen.

WHY DO THE HEATHENS RAGE?

Anti-Semitism, like a haunting shadow, has followed the Jew throughout his weary pilgrimage. But today the Jew is more vulnerable than ever to some of its corrosive effects on his morale. What must he do to stand erect?

Preached on Shabbat Zachor, 1943

6

Why Do the Heathens Rage?

THE Sabbath of Remembrance, *Shabbat Zachor*, derives its name from the first word of the *Maftir* appended to the biblical reading of this morning, the Sabbath preceeding Purim. Actually, the added portion deals with Amalek's attack upon Israel at least 1000 years before the Purim episode. But the spiritual resemblance between Amalek and Haman was so striking that our sages also attributed to Haman the questionable distinction of being a physical descendant of Amalek. Thus, the two narratives are linked not only by the similarity of motifs but also by the blood kinship that bound the respective villains. This two-fold association gives the morning's additional reading special relevance.

But Zachor does more than merely underscore the Purim theme. It invests Purim with spiritual significance. Haman's attempts to destroy Israel thus becomes a phase of the recurrent struggle of Amalek against God: *Milchamah la-Adonoy b'Amalek midor dor*, the enemy of Israel versus the Rock of Israel. Thus, Zachor reminds us that we Jews suffer not only for what we are and cannot help being, but also for what we represent.

It was in this light that our ancestors always regarded persecution. When the heathens assembled in battle-array against Israel, they were actually raging against God, "against the Lord and His anointed." Israel was being singled out for persecution because it represented God's truth. It was this knowledge which girded our ancestors to face trial and humiliation with unyielding courage. They derived added strength from their whole-hearted acceptance of the tradition they represented. They did not suffer

45

for a burden imposed by destiny but for a way of life with which they gladly identified themselves. They suffered proudly for a cause worth the suffering. Thus they were insulated against the shocks of a hostile environment.

Today, however, the suffering of most of our people is especially pathetic. Gone, first of all, is the awareness of the true reason for our suffering. We do not discern in our problem any spiritual dimensions. We do not realize that we are being assaulted for the ideals we represent. Anti-Semitism does not awaken in us any dignity or self-respect. On the contrary, it is accompanied by the pathological development in many Jews of a feeling of inferiority, of self-contempt. Many have actually begun to believe that we do in large measure correspond to the fantastic image of us that Hitler has created. The fact of persecution itself has become valid proof of our guilt.

Many of us do not suffer for a cause which we claim as our own. We suffer for what we cannot help being. This intensifies the suffering. It is already a commonplace observation that the spiritually disfranchized German Jews suffered most humiliation and shame under Hitler. Theirs was a tragedy devoid of the elements of grandeur and dignity which alone redeem tragedy. Our sages spoke of them when they asked: "When do the evil decrees of the pagans against Israel succeed?" "When Israel casts away the Torah," was the answer. Pagan decrees are most effective against the Jews who spurn their heritage. Amalek is most successful against the stragglers in our midst. ". . . he met thee by the way and smote the hindmost of thee, all that were enfeebled in thy rear."

The first task that confronts us therefore is to discover the true nature of modern anti-Semitism, to see it as an attempt to crush the ideals we represent. Unfortunately, most students of the problem have failed to recognize the spiritual issues involved in it. The problem of the Jewish minority is usually considered as a part of the larger problem of all minorities. The Jews are said to suffer from the ordinary prejudices to which all minority groups are heir—namely, the dislike for the unlike or the need

46

for a whipping-boy in times of personal and national frustration. The Jews constitute a convenient object of vicarious punishment.

There are, besides, it is claimed, additional irritants to account for the hostility against the Jews. The fact of being different would by itself be enough to invite suspicion, fear, and hatred. But in addition, they differ in two such basic and vital respects as religion and ethnic origin. Haman's accusation against the Jews of Shushan was simply that "their laws are different from all other peoples." This renders them heir to a double portion of unpopularity. Moreover, in the Christian myth, the Jew plays the part of the arch villain, the deicide. Then there is the fact that unlike any other minority group, the Jew is ubiquitous both in time and space. This renders him easily available. And he is also quite conspicuous. This makes him most exposed to attack. Finally, having no strong nation to protect him or a state to intervene in his behalf, he is totally defenseless.

Because of all these reasons, it is maintained, anti-Semitism undoubtedly differs from other cases of group hostility. But it differs only in intensity, in degree. It does not differ in kind.

Yet, after all this is said, there are certain aspects of anti-Semitism which remain unaccounted for. Maurice Samuel in "The Great Hatred," has very lucidly and penetratingly focused attention upon them. In the first place, while ordinary group prejudices are characterized by feelings of "distaste, distrust and sometimes contempt, anti-Semitism is markedly noted by fear, convulsive horror and vast delusions of persecution." Against the ordinary conviction of superiority that accompanies group hostility, anti-Semitism betrays in the persecutor a cringing inferiority complex. Secondly, there is the mad disparity between the actual proportion of Jewish participation in contemporaneous Western life and the wide extent of the world's preoccupation with the Jews. "How shall we explain the related phenomenon, the obsessional exaggeration of Jewish numbers, Jewish financial and political power and Jewish unity of purpose which seeks to justify this preoccupation?"

These compelling considerations lead Samuel to conclude that anti-Semitism is indeed a unique phenomenon. It is directed against the spiritual ideals the Jew represents—ideals that Fascism must destroy or be destroyed by. Thus, fundamentally, it is not the Jew whom the dictators fear, but Judaism. Again we are involved in the war of Amalek against God.

And it is interesting to note that not only Samuel, but non-Jewish thinkers as well have discerned, although from different approaches, the prominent role that hatred for Judaism plays in the hatred for the Jew. Thus, we hear John MacMurray saying in "The Clue to History": "Fascism discovers that the source of all this pressure towards progress, equality, freedom, and common humanity is the Jew. . . . It is the truth. Hitler's declaration that the Jewish consciousness is poison to the Aryan race is the deepest insight that the Western world has yet achieved into its own nature. . . . It is the Jewish consciousness which is the enemy. . . . It is the hidden penetration of the Jewish spirit into the Gentile mind that is the danger. . . . At all costs the leaven must be gotten out of the lump or very soon the whole world will be leavened and the result will be the final end of the 'Aryan' (sic pagan) tradition."

Jacques Maritain, the profoundest contemporary Catholic mind, expresses in semi-mystical, but no less pointed words, the same insight: "The diverse specific causes which the observer may assign to anti-Semitism" he says, "mask an underlying spring of hatred deeper down. If the world hates the Jew, it is because the world detests their passion for the absolute. . . . It is the vocation of Israel which the world execrates."

All these modern thinkers are endorsing an insight our sages glimpsed long ago. Noting the similarity between the Hebrew words *Sinai* and *Sinah* (hatred) they established a causal relationship between the two. It was because of *Sinai*, because of the truths revealed and accepted there, that hatred for the Jew came into being. Anti-Semitism is thus at bottom an expression of anti-Sinaism.

Let us proceed now a step further to examine briefly the ideals which we represent and our enemies fear. Which are the doctrines that impel Fascism, instinctively, to sense that the Jewish tradition is the *"s'or she-b'isa*, the leaven in the lump," which must be destroyed if the Nazi philosophy is to prevail?

We will find that these two sets of beliefs clash violently in their attitudes towards God, humanity and man. You cannot reconcile the God of the moral law who requires of man justice and mercy, who redeems the oppressed, who commands: "do not despoil the poor because he is poor," with the Aryan god of power who regards the very fact of weakness as justification for destruction. From the mouths of German babes and sucklings we can hear nursery rhymes such as the one which glorifies the big fly who caught a smaller one:

> " 'Please' begged the victim, 'let me go
> For I am such a little foe.'
> 'No,' said the victor 'not at all,
> For I am big and you are small.' "

You cannot reconcile a belief in humanity which affirms the unity of all mankind, the equality of all groups, the rights of every people to its independent existence, with the racial myth which not only creates the allegedly superior Aryan race but also endows it with the right to subjugate and exploit all "inferior" ones. You cannot reconcile the attitude which looks upon man, each man, as a child of God, endowed with sanctity, possessing rights that are uncompromisingly his, with the frenzied declaration of Hitler: "Man is congenitally evil. . . . To govern him everything is permissable. You must lie, betray, even kill when policy demands it." No, one or the other philosophy must perish, which shall it be? Anti-Semitism is Hitler's way of answering.

A true understanding of why the heathens rage, should therefore help us first of all to know ourselves, to know what we symbolize. We are not despised for what we are or fail to be but for the spiritual ideals that have become associated with the name *Jew*. This realization is essential for our psychic wellbeing. It will restore our corroded dignity and self-respect. It

49

will also dispel many an illusion in the confused minds of our assimilationist Jews who have been arguing from the implied major premise that we are like other minorities, only more so. They will come to understand that the problem of anti-Semitism is not to be solved by dissolving the Jews. They will realize that any person, Jew or otherwise, who championed life's spiritual values would incur the wrath of the heathen. In that light will they understand why Fascism which began ostensibly as a crusade against the Jew, has now turned against democracy, the political embodiment of the ideals we represent, and why, Roosevelt, the staunch representative of these ideals, has been re-Christened (or should we say de-Christened?) "Rosenfeld." They will perhaps even come to feel that for the Jew to be singled out by Nazism as its most implacable foe is in itself a glorious tribute. A man may also be known by the enemies he makes. To really know ourselves and what we represent is to be freed from many a psychosis and to replace it with a sense of pride.

But merely to know that we suffer for what we represent is not enough unless at the same time we accept what we represent. To suffer for a spiritual heritage with which we are associated by our persecutors, in spite of ourselves, to endure persecution for what we cannot help being, is to court psychic disaster. For then we dissipate our moral energies in perpetual rebellion against our fate and we thereby further weaken our resistance to the attack. If we are to face the challenge as our ancestors did, with courage and determination, we must identify ourselves with what we actually represent.

What does that involve? It involves firstly, living according to the ideals that derive from our beliefs concerning God, humanity and personality. These must be translated into a program for Jewish life. If we conceive God as a God of mercy and the redeemer of the oppressed, how can we better attest to that belief than by contributing to those charitable institutions which support the fallen, care for the aged, feed the hungry and shelter the refugee? If our belief in humanity is such as affirms the equality and the rights of all peoples, how can we better attest

50

to this belief than by helping our own people to live independently and creatively on its ancient soil? If we regard man as endowed with sanctity and an inviolable personality, how can we better attest to that belief than by supporting those institutions that help defend the Jew and his rights against those who would deprive him of them. Only in such ways does our identification with the ideals we represent become real.

Secondly, identification with what we represent involves accepting our Jewish heritage—the context in which our ideals find their meaning. Let us, as our ancestors did, utilize our spiritual armor to shield us against the shafts of persecution. Let us, as our ancestors did, derive that inner fortitude which comes only from a whole-hearted acceptance of Judaism.

By this two-fold action we shall not only rob persecution of its sting, but we shall at the same time clothe life with richness and dignity. We shall derive spiritual sustenance from our ancient ritual. We shall draw upon Israel's legacy for what we need of strength of character and enhancement of personal life. We shall enjoy the spiritual fellowship of Moses, Jeremiah, Akiba and the Baal Shem Tov. We shall experience a feeling of life's holiness by communion with God. We shall share a faith so dynamic and so ennobling that when suffering comes, if come it must, it appears to be only a small price to pay for a priceless heritage.

At this critical juncture in our historical odyssey, a special duty devolves upon the American Jewish community. For one, we have most at stake. The foe threatens our democracy and our religion at once. Patriotism and piety therefore reinforce each other in impelling us to accept the challenge heroically. This war against Amalek for the sake of God, finds us doubly dedicated. Secondly, because we American Jews enjoy greater strength, freedom and means than any other section of world Jewry, we are especially committed to an active part in our people's destiny. Mordecai might well charge us today as he did Esther: "Who knows but for just such a time as this hast thou attained thy royal estate."

As we are preparing to celebrate the deliverance of Purim, we find ourselves confronted by an enemy infinitely more cruel than Haman. An hour of trial has once again struck on our historic clock. Our national memories should inspire us with the realization that we have survived many lethal blows. With the inspiration that our heroic past provides, with the wisdom that self-knowledge endows and with the strength that accepting our destiny affords, let us so discharge our divine duty that our children and our children's children will be able to point to us, their ancestors, and say: "In a dark hour of crisis our fathers saw the light and followed it."

THE BOOK OF THE LIVING

Whether we are aware of it or not, our actions are perpetually making vital indelible entries in a variety of human volumes. It is therefore of crucial significance that we pay prayerful attention to the quality of our deeds.

Preached on Rosh Hashanah, 1952

7

The Book of the Living

A few months ago I read a slim, sensitive volume entitled: "Rise Up and Walk," by one Turnley Walker. In it he describes his dreadful encounter with polio which struck him down in his middle thirties. He sketches the delirium of pain and fear, the sense of guilt over creating massive expenses while helpless to provide income for his wife and children, the initial loss of faith in ever writing the book he was just about to begin. He succeeds in conveying the feeling of disaster of a young man who suddenly realizes that he no longer has control over his pain-racked limbs. His bed is a "pit of helplessness,"—walking, "a forgotten miracle." Slowly and marvelously his motion is restored to him and the book is abundant proof that he has been left with no emotional or mental scars.

Now, in the book, Mr. Walker describes not only his personal reactions but also those of his two fellow sufferers on either side similarly afflicted. The 37 year old lawyer on one side sobbing in bed and whispering "God I'm scared"; the successful manufacturer on the other side also grappling with fear, defeatism, despair.

After I finished reading the book a curious, though irrelevant, thought came to me. It took the form of a question. "How," I asked myself, "would the lawyer and the manufacturer have behaved if they had known that Walker was going to record their behavior in a book? What if they had realized that their every reaction and outcry and exclamation and conversation were being written down for all the world to read? Would they have been more courageous, more trusting, more hopeful?"

As these questions punctuated my thinking I suddenly realized that they were prompted by a comment of our sages which I had read some time previous. It was related to the biblical story of Joseph and his brothers. We recall that when the brothers saw the proud, tale-bearing Joseph approaching thcm in the fields, they plotted at once to kill him. But Reuben, the oldest, wanted to save Joseph. And so Reuben counsels his brothers not to kill him but rather to cast him into the pit. Reuben had planned to return after his brother's departure, to rescue Joseph and to bring him home. We know of course that when Reuben later returns to the pit, he discovers to his great dismay that Joseph is gone. It is upon this incident that our rabbis comment: "If Reuben realized that the Torah was recording his every deed he would have picked Joseph up bodily and he would have carried him home to his father." He would not have resorted to subterfuges or schemes. He would have said to his brothers: "Be men, be human. After all he is only a spoiled child. That's not how brother treats brother. And if not for his sake, then think of father. How dare we even entertain such a thought? I'm taking Joseph home now—and don't anybody try to stop me!"

Yes, Reuben, that's how you might have spoken. That's the speech you might have delivered if you had only realized that your deeds were being written down for all generations to read. You would not have resorted to chance. You would have shown a manhood worthy of the occasion. You would have been more outspoken, more courageous. If you had only known. . . .

This then was the origin of the questions which came to me after finishing Mr. Walker's book. What if the lawyer and the manufacturer realized that their deeds were being written up for all to read?

From here let me now carry this question closer home. What if we realized, every one of us, that someone around us was writing a book about us— recording our every action in our places of business, in our offices, in our homes, in our places of amusement and recreation? What if we knew that someone was noting, for all to read, our relationship to our subordinates, our loyalty to our mates, our faithfulness to truth, our response to charitable appeals, our obedience to justice? How would we behave? What if we suddenly realized that the curtain of secrecy and privacy had been ripped away and instead the full glare of the public spotlight was turned relentlessly upon us and exposing us constantly to view?

I suppose most of us will say: Fortunately that possibility is only the product of the rabbi's morbid imagination. That's a frightening thought which happily is unrelated to reality.

Dear friends, on Rosh Hashanah let us face the challenging truth that what I have been describing is not an imaginative fantasy but a striking fact. Whether we like it or not, whether we are aware of it or not, everything that we do is written down indelibly in the record. And I mean this not only in the theological sense in which Rabbi Akiba taught and Judaism believed: that our actions are part of the Divine record. I mean more specifically that everything we do is written down in the human record—becomes a vital part of somebody's book of life.

During these High Holy Days we repeat often the prayer that we may be inscribed " B'sefer Hachayim—In the book of life." The word "Hachayim" is usually rendered "life." But it also means "the living." "Sefer Hachayim," would then mean, "the book of the living." If we understand it in this sense, then we grasp the truth which I have tried to underscore. Whether we like it or not, we are being written up in a book, in many books. Our actions are shaping human biographies, are being imprinted on living parchment, are being woven into the plots and dramas of human destiny.

Most of us enjoy the great privilege and the greater responsibility of parenthood. How often do we pause to realize that we are daily making indelible entries into our children's book of life? Do we fully appreciate how responsive our children are to our influences and how enduring these influences prove to be?

Luther Burbank the famous scientist and botanist pointed out that metals are the hardest things to change. They require tremendous force to mold them. To change gold you must use a

57

heavy hammer. Gold will resist acids and oxidation. To change iron you have to use tremendous heat and outside influences of every type. A plant will respond to the most delicate outside forces. But the most sensitive thing of all is a child. A child will respond to a thousand outside forces which neither a plant nor a metal will feel. Therefore, it is we whose deeds are being inscribed boldly between the covers of our children's book of life. This truth is attested to by every autobiography.

Chaim Nachman Bialik was considered until his death in 1934 the Hebrew poet laureate. In one of his very touching poems he tries to trace to its origin the sigh, the *krechtz* which is so frequently heard in his poems. And he tells us how in his childhood, his widowed mother would slave in the market place by day and toil with her domestic chores at home late into the night. Long after she thought all her children were asleep, she would be sewing and baking. Little Chaim in his bed overheard her unanswered protests to the Almighty and could hear her tears rolling into the dough that she was kneading for tomorrow's bread. When she served her family the warm bread on the following morning, Bialik says, he ate it and with it there entered into his bones his mother's tears and her sighs. Unbeknown to her, of course, she was making decisive imprints on little Chaim's scroll of life that no subsequent experience could eradicate.

If we ourselves paused briefly to trace back the significant passages in our personal autobiographies to their source, would we not find that much of the authorship was done by our parents. And if a trained analyst would apply his magnifying glass to our book of life he would find even more than we recognize. The most vital passages in our book of life would be traced back to our first and most persistent heroes—our parents.

Charles Francis Potter in his book, "The Preacher and I," makes this interesting comment: "A eulogy is customary which is a sort of laudatory biography. But I am always aware when listening to the remarks of the mourners and looking into their thoughtful faces that the true life story of the deceased, including his mistakes as well as his good deeds, is engraved deep in the memory of his friends and that he wrote it there himself."

If we move a bit further with this thought we realize that it is not only in the books of the lives of those dearest to us that we make vital entries. The pen of our deeds often leaves its lasting sketches on the volumes of casual acquaintances or even total strangers. Open up your own book of life and read. Did the teacher who awakened within you a love for literature realize how significant a passage she was writing? Did the hero who conquered his severe handicap appreciate how much courage he gave you to surmount your own? Did the anonymous Jews who purchased Jewish survival with their lives realize how deeply their deed etched itself onto the impressionable slate of your soul?

In his book "The Bond Between Us," Dr. Loomis relates a significant personal experience. Shortly after he settled in California his wife died of pneumonia. Within the next few days, three doctors came individually to console him. Each of them gave him a blank check to fill in any amount he needed and to return the sum whenever he became affluent enough to do so. In recalling the incident, Dr. Loomis writes: "This act in a way prompted every decent thing I have done in all the years since."

This, then, is a basic truth of human experience. Whether we like it or not we are being inscribed B'sefer Hachayim—in the book of the living. In the biographies of our loved ones and fellow-men, in the ledger of the general community, in the chronicles of Judaism—we are constantly making entries. What kind of entries am I making?—this might well be the question with which we ought to begin and end every God-given day.

Let us consider some specific areas of our lives against the background of this truth. At the White House Conference on Child Study there were listed nineteen requirements, the first of which reads: "For every child, spiritual and moral training to help him stand firm under the pressure of life." Are we providing our children with a training which is equal to and stronger than the pressure of life today? Have we succeeded in creating a spiritual climate in the home through the practice of *Tsedakah*, the observance of Jewish ritual, the reading of uplifting books, the playing of ennobling music, and above all by treating one another with kindness and warm regard? Someone once said "My religion is my mother." Are we, through our personal behavior, helping to make religion real to our children? Are we living the truths upon which we want them to build their lives? What kind of entries are we making in our children's Book of Life?

As Americans we must also ask ourselves a series of important questions. The ledger of Democracy is the sum total of the lines contributed by each of its citizens—whether they be occupants of high political office or humble workers in a factory or on a farm. Each of us makes a contribution to the volume of America. What kind of passages are we writing?

Are we practicing the slogans of brotherhood and tolerance which we urge upon the Protestant majority in our dealings with the Negro minority?

We are all quick to recite the freedoms which, as Americans, we enjoy. But are we as prone to accept the responsibilities these freedoms involve? Are we using freedom of conscience to conscientiously seek the truth so that we may do it? Are we using our freedom of speech to speak out fearlessly in behalf of justice when it is violated? Are we using our freedom of thought especially in this presidential election year to think straight and hard about the fundamental issues so that our ballot may be cast with intelligence? Are we using our freedom of worship to strengthen the will to worship in ourselves and in those about us? Are we sufficiently dedicated to "free enterprise," to give up willingly a portion of our enterprise to secure freedom at home and abroad?

Do we appreciate the fact that the word "bless" and the word "bleed" come from the same root and thereby remind us that our American blessings were dearly purchased? Do we act as though we realized that we can not preserve our Bill of Rights unless we are prepared to pay our bill of duties? What kind of entries are we making in America's Book of Life?

Lastly, let us consider our contribution to Judaism. Here, too, we must realize that the ultimate story will be the sum total of the individual paragraphs we each insert.

There was a time when we indulged ourselves in the comforting illusions that we could afford to let our rabbis worry about preserving and observing Judaism while the laymen went their merry ways. Today we know better. Today we realize that in order for the narrative of Judaism in America to be inspiring and significant, each Jew must write a meaningful passage. The story cannot be "ghost" written.

Well, what kind of passages are we each writing? Is Judaism to us like a woman in the ballad "a sometime thing?" Do we take it with us into our offices, our places of business, into the market-place and make known our Jewishness through honest dealings and integrity? Are we using the vast leisure at our command, more than employed men have ever known, to inform ourselves about the unequalled heritage of Judaism, to enrich the communal institutions with our voluntary efforts?

Are we using the vast resources of the richest Jewish community in our history to strengthen our Seminaries and schools of Jewish learning and to support the third Jewish commonwealth in Israel through the purchase of bonds?

Are we availing ourselves fully of the opportunities for spiritual growth and weekly recreation which our Synagogue and Shabbat offer?

What kind of entries are we making in the Jewish Book of Life?

The American poet-philosopher, George Santayana, once wrote that "we commit the blotted manuscript of our lives more willingly to the flames when we find the immortal text half engrossed in a fairer copy." On this Rosh Hashanah let us resolve to live with the constant awareness that our every deed is being inscribed on human parchment. We may never write a line which is printed but we are all the authors of vital passages in living volumes. Let us strive to make "fairer copy." Let us so live that whatever text we inscribe in the *Sefer Hachayim*, the Book of the living shall be "*L'maancha Elohim Chayim*—For Thy sake, O God of Life." Amen.

WHAT IS MAN THAT THOU ART MINDFUL OF HIM?

This effort to appraise Man, was made during the Nazi era which witnessed the most shocking human depravity in recorded history. Its conclusions are still relevant—and indispensible—if we are to leave our children a better world than we found.

Preached on Rosh Hashanah, 1943

8

What Is Man That Thou Art Mindful of Him?

IT is said that when Professor Elliot was president of Harvard University, he once had occasion to dedicate a new hall of philosophy and he was searching for an appropriate inscription to place above its entrance. For that purpose he called his faculty members together and after much deliberation, they suggested the well-known Greek maxim: "Man is the measure of all things." With that they adjourned for their summer vacation. When school reopened in the fall, they were surprised to find that the president had decided upon his own inscription. Instead of "Man is the measure of all things," he had seen fit to have inscribed, "What is man that Thou art mindful of him?"

Professor Elliot, of course, had quoted from the 8th Psalm where the psalmist in a moment of awe at the majestic splendor of the universe calls out: "When I behold Thy heavens, the work of Thy fingers, the moon and the stars which Thou hast established, what is man that Thou art mindful of him and the son of man that Thou thinkest of him?" When Professor Elliot chose that inscription over the one suggested by his colleagues, he indicated that he was not quite so certain about his faith in man as to make him the measure of all things. He had a far more humble estimate of man's significance.

This raises for us what I regard to be a central problem not only in religion, but in all our thinking and especially in our planning for the future. The type of society we are envisioning must depend very intimately upon what we think of man who is going to live in it, whether we think it is going to be inhabited by man, the child of God, or man, the brother of the beast.

To be sure, the psalmist's question, "What is man that Thou art mindful of him?" has today been punctuated by a larger and more challenging question mark than when it was first uttered.

Astronomy has magnified the question mark. The psalmist in his day had a very limited idea about the real size of this universe of ours. He could only behold the heavens, the moon and the stars with the naked eye, and to the naked eye a maximum of 8,000 stars are visible. Today, however, when thanks to the telescope and modern astronomy we realize that our whole solar system is but an insignificant and inconsequential planet whirling about in an almost infinite sea of space, today the question is especially crushing. In a universe so staggering in size, "What is man that Thou art mindful of him?"

Science has magnified the question mark. Science looks at man quantitatively, the sum total of some tissues, cells, liquids, chemicals, some gray matter called the brain, plus some other ingredients. Thus, an English scientist informs us that a man weighing 140 lbs. contains enough fat for 7 cakes of soap, enough carbon for 9,000 pencils, phosphorous to make 2200 match heads, magnesium for one dose of salt, iron for one medium-sized nail, lime to white wash a chicken-coop, sulphur to rid one dog of fleas and enough water to fill a 10 gallon barrel—net value about 98 cents. "What is man that Thou art mindful of him?"

Industry has magnified the question mark. It has depersonalized man, robbed him of his distinctively human characteristics and reduced him to the level of a mechanical cog in an indifferent and colossal machine. When we see man enslaved to steel, mastered by the very tools he has created, "What is man that Thou art mindful of him?"

But most of all man himself has magnified the question mark. Man seems to have shrunk not only physically but spiritually as well. "Man, biologically considered . . ." William James observed, "is the most formidable of all beasts of prey and, indeed, the only one that preys systematically on its own species." The melancholy truth of these words is being demonstrated today in its full tragic dimensions. When we behold man desperately engaged once again in a titanic struggle to destroy himself, when we see "nazified" man indulging in wholesale murder of mothers and children, suffocating thousands in cattle cars, injecting innocent victims with fatal diseases—"What is man that Thou art mindful of him?"

This then is the dilemma facing all thinking men. What shall be the inscription on our wall? With what philosophy of man shall we face the future? What does our religion have to say about this crucial question?

Throughout our religious literature there are occasional expressions of disappointment in man. Among our sages there sometimes could be heard the same type of disagreement that obtained between Professor Elliot and his colleagues. Thus, we hear two divergent views as to why man was created last in the order of creation. One sage attributes the reason to man's supreme significance. "Just as a mortal king when he invites someone very dear to visit him, prepares an elaborate meal and comfortable sleeping quarters for his guest, and only when these are prepared does he summon his guest, so too, God first prepared food and shelter; that is, He created the grass, vegetables, trees, animals and only then on the sixth day when all was in readiness, did He invite his beloved guest, man, to come and partake of this glory." The other sage says no! Man's late creation is a sign of his insignificance. "Man was the last of creation so that, should he become proud and inflated, he may be reminded that the flea preceded him in the order of creation."

Yet, in spite of such occasional expressions of doubt in man's value and importance, there can be no question that one of the basic principles of our faith is belief in man as having been created in the image of God. Yes, man's origin is from the lowly earth but at creation God breathed His Divine Spirit into him and that spirit became his patent of nobility. In fact, even the psalmist who asks, "What is man that Thou art mindful of him, and the son of man that Thou takest account of him?" goes on

65

immediately to say: "Nevertheless, Thou hast made him but little lower than the angels."

Now let us make no mistake about it. This psalmist was no blind optimist. Neither was he a cloistered student who had his nose so deeply buried in his scrolls that his eye could not reach beyond the parchment. He was very much a part of the life about him. True he hardly suspected the real size of this immense universe but even with the naked eye the world looks tremendous enough and man proportionately microscopic. He also saw men exploited as though they were tools, and ground to the dust as though they were stones. He knew of the heartlessness of a Pharoah, the malicious plotting of a Haman, the ruthlessness of a Nebuchadnezzar. He tasted personal suffering and humiliation at the hands of man. Thus we hear him cry out "*Eli, Eli, lamah azavtani*—My God, my God why hast Thou forsaken me? I am a worm and no man, a reproach of men and despised of the people. All that see me laugh me to scorn." It was such a man who made the tremendous declaration of faith in man: "Nevertheless, Thou hast made him but little lower than the angels."

This does not mean, of course, that we believe man to be infallible. What we do believe is that man is potentially good, and though he may sin, he does not obliterate the divine element within him. I am told that the bricks used in Babylon for public buildings were always stamped with the king's image. In a museum, however, there is one brick where the footprints of a dog who probably trampled on the brick while it was still wet, nearly effaces the image of the king. Man is made, we believe, in God's image even though his soul sometimes becomes smudged with the footprints of an animal. He possesses latent good, the divine spark that can be fanned into flames.

Difficult though this faith may be, it is indispensable to any hopes for progress in human betterment. Unless we believe in man's potential goodness and divine character, we have neither reason to believe in his ability to govern himself wisely nor to respect his rights. How can we plan for a free world unless we are convinced that man can prize freedom and use it to promote happiness? Democracy has this faith in man. It declares: "We take these truths to be self-evident, that all men are created equal and are endowed by their Creator with certain inalienable rights, that among these rights are life, liberty and the pursuit of happiness." Notice Democracy does not try to prove man's rights. It calls them "self-evident truths"—a non-theological expression for "faith." Because democracy has this faith in man, it permits him to determine for himself who shall rule him and how, what, if anything, he will believe, how and when he shall speak.

Fascism does not have this faith in man. Otto Strasser in "Hitler and I," quotes the mad prophet of Nazism as saying, "From this conviction I will never depart. . . . Man is congenitally evil. He can only be controlled by force. To govern him everything is permissable. You must lie, betray, even kill, when policy demands it." Notice again, Hitler does not attempt to prove the grounds for his lack of faith in man. He calls it a conviction from which he will never depart. His lack of faith in man is also a matter of faith. And because Nazism does not believe in man, it determines who will rule him and how, what he will believe and think, what and when he will speak. It determines also if and how he shall live. In the final analysis therefore, whether we believe in man or not, determines whether man shall be free or enslaved, whether we shall march ahead or revert to the savage.

There is still another reason why this faith in man is so vital. Unless we believe in the good in ourselves we shall never realize it. The surest way of becoming moral failures is to convince ourselves that we can never overcome our moral shortcomings. A bad child becomes worse when he finally begins to believe his elders who say he is bad and a first offender frequently becomes a hardened criminal because he becomes convinced of the truth of society's opinion of him. Conversely, the successful human counsellor is the one who can take hold of a defeated and frustrated person and convince him of his own latent powers and abilities. The only way to bring out the best in ourselves is to believe that it is there and that we are but little lower than the angels.

67

But how are we to develop this faith in man's divinity, the faith in man's potential goodness? True, this faith may be necessary for moral progress. It may be indispensable for our own spiritual development. Yet how can we maintain it when it seems to fly in the face of all experience?

In the first place, I think, when we are about to despair in man let us realize how far he *has* developed and in how short a time. To get a vivid picture of human achievement in its proper perspective, let us compress all of man's history into twelve hours —the time it takes the small hand on our watches to make a complete revolution. Well, if we did that, it would take until a quarter to twelve before man abandoned his habits of a wandering hunter and became domesticated. At seven minutes to twelve man would learn how to write. At three minutes to twelve he would hear the Ten Commandments. And at a few seconds before twelve he would be sitting in Independence Hall drawing up the Declaration of Independence.

When we look at man in this light, we see that spiritually he is still in his infancy. He is only now beginning to walk and how depressed we are when we see him fall, thinking in our impatience, that he will never be able to walk at all. The truth is that, for an infant, clap hands! He is walking very well. Perhaps in terms of what still remains to be done man has yet a long way to go, but in terms of what he has already accomplished, he has indeed negotiated a most impressive distance.

There is still another source of faith that we can tap. When we look out at the world scene we tend to be distracted primarily by "man's inhumanity to man." We see only the wicked men, the brutal men who cause war and capture the headlines. We tend to overlook the plain, simple, honest and good people, the countless millions who abhor war and pray for peace, the men and women of genuine goodness who never get into the newspapers at all because there is nothing sensational about a man sacrificing everything to give his children those things he never had, or a man working selflessly in a laboratory to cut down disease and death, or a man supporting his aged parents, or a

68

man honestly tilling his soil and eating and sharing the fruits of his labors. In times of war we develop a blind spot for the good men do and we see only the evil.

Yes, this war has produced some horrible examples of man's brutality. But it has also given us the story of the four chaplains who instinctively surrendered their own life-belts to some soldiers when their boat was torpedoed and went down to a watery grave while praying below deck. It has also given us the story of the anonymous underground workers who at the risk of death, smuggled in arms to the Jews in the Warsaw ghetto with which the latter made as inspiring a last stand as was ever made by any hopelessly outnumbered army. And the numbers are legion of those unconquerable souls in the occupied lands who are daily risking their all to keep alive the flame of liberty and hope.

In the final analysis, therefore, our faith in man depends upon which experiences of man we consider. We recall that in Saroyan's "The Human Comedy," little Ulysses is depicted standing on the railroad tracks waving to all who pass on the big, powerful train. All disregard him and his spirits fall. In his own childish world, his faith in man crumbles. But then a Negro hobo on the platform of the last car, sees Ulysses wave and not only waves back to him, but also sings him a song telling him that he is going home. Ever after Ulysses goes through life thinking not of the men who destroyed his faith but of the singing hitch-hiker who rebuilt it.

We can go through life thinking of either picture. We can think of those who destroy our faith in man, but if we do so we become bitter, we despair, we surrender all possibilities of advancement. On the other hand we can think of those who answer our call, those who restore our faith in man and in ourselves. If we think of these we are encouraged, we are inspired and we capture the faith by which we must live and grow.

In the new year that lies ahead, let us not be dismayed by man's failures but inspired by his triumphs so that like the psalmist of old, we too will say: "Thou hast made him but

69

little lower than the angels." And like the modern Hebrew poet, Tchernichowsky, we too will sing:

> "Laugh at my dreams my dearest,
> Laugh and I repeat anew,
> That I still believe in man
> As I still believe in you.
>
> For my soul is yet unsold,
> To the golden calf of scorn,
> And I still believe in man
> And in the spirit in him born."

RIGHTEOUS IN OUR GENERATION

The achievements of each Jewish generation must be measured against the background of its own circumstances. How do we measure up?

Preached on Shabbat Noach, 1951

TO **Ds**

DATE 9-6-89 TIME 11—

While You Were Out

M *Larry Timbow*

OF

PHONE (A/C   )

NUMBER   EXTENSION

TELEPHONED	✓	**PLEASE CALL**	✓	
CALLED TO SEE YOU		**WILL CALL AGAIN**		
WANTS TO SEE YOU		**URGENT**		
RETURNED YOUR CALL				

MESSAGE

CALL TAKEN BY

9

Righteous in Our Generation

PEOPLE who are seriously engaged in any worth-while enterprise pause, periodically, to take inventory. They evaluate their progress to date and chart their prospects for the future.

Such an inventory is in fact taking place today in the American Zionist movement and I feel that every intelligent synagogue-minded Jew ought to be taking spiritual inventory into the enterprise called *Judaism*.

This soul-searching endeavor deserves top priority on the agenda of every Jew in whose heart there stirs a love for the heritage of his fathers and a concern to transmit it to his children. How are things in our spiritual household today? What may we expect tomorrow? Growth or decay? Survival or disappearance? What is the prospect which faces American Judaism?

It must be admitted, dear friends, that this question has already been considered by many thoughtful Jews and that the answer has been far from unanimous. Indeed, the difference of opinion has been very profound, as profound as the one which divided Rabbi Yochanan and Resh Lakish in one of the best known talmudic controversies. Their controversy is relevant to our inquiry.

We will recall that the Torah in its description of Noah said of him, "Noah was a righteous man; he was upright in his generation." To our sages the word *b'dorotav*—in his generation— seemed superfluous. The Torah might very well have omitted it. It could have simply recorded: "Noah was a righteous man; he was upright." Why *b'dorotav*? Why that qualification?

It was this word that precipitated the debate between the two great rabbinic authorities of the third century over Noah's

true stature and worth. Rabbi Yochanan saw in the word b'dorotav a reservation on the part of the Torah. "In his generation,"
he appeared like a righteous man. Living as he did among brutal,
pitiless men, men who deserved no better fate than the flood—
among them Noah appeared like a tsadik. Had he lived in Abraham's time, however, Noah would have been a spiritual non-
entity, a moral nobody. Thus, says Rabbi Yochanan, the Torah
actually damned Noah by faint praise.

Resh Lakish interpreted the word, b'dorotav, quite otherwise.
Imagine! he said, even in his generation—surrounded as he was
by corruption and rottenness—even there he maintained his integrity, his decency. How difficult it must have been to remain
an island of righteousness in a sea of wickedness. It would have
been so natural, so understandable if he had permitted himself
to be submerged, if he had yielded, if he had surrendered to his
environment. But he did not yield! The Torah, therefore, cli-
maxed its tribute to Noah when it reminded us that he was a
righteous man in an unrighteous generation.

Historically, it is very significant that this charitable view of
Noah came from Resh Lakish. For he spoke out of the depths
of personal experience. The Talmud tells us that Resh Lakish
had not always been a student and teacher of the tradition. Big
and powerful Resh Lakish had in fact been alternately a circus
performer and a highway man. The company he had kept had
not been of the finest. It was through a chance meeting with
Rabbi Yochanan that he was persuaded to marry Rabbi Yochanan's
sister and to dedicate his strength to the discipline of study. Later
he grew into the intellectual equal of his brother-in-law.

He never forgot, however, what association with wickedness
could do to a man, how an unfavorable environment takes its
toll on a man's character and ideals. If in spite of everything and
everyone around him, Noah had the courage to remain uncom-
promised, Ah, here was moral grandeur indeed!

I cannot help but hear, in this controversy between the two
sages over the character of Noah, a foreshadowing of the contemporary conflicting estimates of the stature of the American

Jew. In appraising the American Jew and his Judaism, his achievements to date, his possibilities for the future, there are differences as deep as those which divided Rabbi Yochanan and Resh Lakish.

Who among us has not heard Rabbi Yochanan's verdict? His opinion is usually expressed by the old-timer—the Jew who remembers Judaism as it was lived in the ghetto, who prefaces all his remarks with: "*Amolige zeiten*, or *Bei unz in der alter haym.*—There was a time . . . , Now, back in the old country. . . ." Turning to the American scene, he shrugs his shoulders disparagingly. "You call these Jews? You call this Judaism? In Kovno, Vilna, Wolozhin—ah, there you had *Yiddishkeit*, there you had Jews!"

"*Shabbos* was *Shabbos*. Not a Jewish wheel turned. Every home was illuminated by candles, every table was decorated with a white cloth, the *challah*, the *kiddush* cup. Every home echoed the prayers, reverberated to the tunes of reverent and joyous *z'miros*. You could feel *Shabbos* wherever you turned. The very air was *Shabbasdig*.

"And *Pesach* . . . for months in advance you could feel its imminence. Before Purim you went to the tailor to begin fitting the annual new suit. You began to press grapes for wine. You began to save chicken fat in special vessels. In a hundred ways you could feel that a special guest was coming to your home. And so with every Jewish holiday.

"Where Jewish learning and scholarship was concerned, even your humblest Jew could quote Scripture and rabbinic sayings. Your homes may have had little furniture but all had a bookcase of Jewish books. Your *Yeshivos* were filled, your houses of study were humming. From early morning until late at night and often even in the hours of darkest night, the sound of learning was never stilled."

Having thus extolled *Yiddishkeit* and *Yiden* in "the old country," it is not very difficult for the old-timer to complete the contrast to the extreme disadvantage of the grandchildren in America.

"*Shabbos* here is the concern of only a handful in a community and all too often a very small handful. *Shabbos* is honored more in the breach than in the observance. Even in heavily populated Jewish neighborhoods you might scarcely know it was *Shabbos* if you did not consult your calendar. Business goes on as usual."

Where Jewish education today is concerned, the old-timer reminds you, where once we had an aristocracy of learning, we have today a democracy of ignorance. Jewish knowledge to any appreciable degree is the possession of a select few, usually only the *K'lay Kodesh*—the so-called "sacred vessels"—the rabbis and the paid religious teachers and functionaries. What was once the common property of every professing Jew is today almost the exclusive domain of the professional Jew. Today we test a pupil of a Hebrew School by opening a *Siddur* to determine whether he can *"daven."* In the Yeshiva we would stick a pin through the pages of a Talmud folio, and there was many a pupil who could tell you by heart every single word that pin pierced on each side of every page.

"This is *Yiddishkeit?*" he asks again despondently. "The milk of Judaism is being cut progressively thinner. After another generation or so, it will be all water, and valueless. *B'dorotav*, in our generation, this is also Judaism. Compared to what was, it is only a shadow of a shadow."

This whole point of view is usually summed up in a disparaging shrug of the shoulders and a deep sigh: *"Es iz America."*

Strangely, the old-timer's pessimistic view of the future of Judaism in America receives support today from an unexpected source—from a segment of the Israeli population.

There has appeared in Israel a school of thought which subscribes to the doctrine of *"shlilat hagolah*—the negation of the diaspora." The subscribers to this viewpoint have written off the possibility of Jewish survival in America. Those who uproot themselves and come to Israel, they say, they will be saved for Jewish life. The remaining Jews in the diaspora, "will fold their tents like the Arabs and silently steal away." They will assimilate, intermarry and disappear.

Nor is this dreary view limited to Israelis. It was most recently expressed by Mr. Edward A. Norman, president of the American Fund for Israel Institutions. Writing in the first issue of American Judaism, Norman said: "In the next few years, few people outside of Israel will care to lead a Jewish life."

He presented the classic argument that a Jewish state was in itself reasonable insurance of Jewish survival and thus removed the principal motivation for Jews remaining Jewish outside of Israel. Very soon American Judaism may be expected to take its last bow and ring down the curtain announcing: "The play is over. The drama of Judaism is at an end." B'dorotav—in our generation, Judaism may still linger. Beyond that it has no life expectancy. Après moi le déluge. After us comes the deluge.

Thus both the old timer and the historical newcomer, the Vilna Jew and the Israeli, dismiss the Judaism of our generation as either a pale and lifeless imitation of a once throbbing civilization or as a withering branch on the Jewish tree of life.

But after both these harsh interpretations of b'dorotav have been heard, Resh Lakish has a word to say. "No! my friends," he protests, "don't be so severe with the American Jew. On the contrary where you find only occasion for despair I find grounds for hope. Where you stand ready to condemn, I am prepared to applaud.

"Do you realize what the American Jew has accomplished b'dorotav—amidst all the obstacles, difficulties and problems of living as a Jew in a non-Jewish environment? Do you realize that living as a Jew in America is often like trying to walk up an escalator which is going down? After all, Old-timer, assuming even that everything you said about the Vilna Jew was true of all Vilna Jews, assuming that you have not become overly romantic by the enchantment which distance lends, what sort of an accomplishment was it for a Jew to observe Shabbos in Vilna? He could scarcely do otherwise! He certainly could not publicly desecrate the Sabbath without exposing himself to overwhelming public scorn and indignation. In Vilna a Jew would have found it more difficult not to observe the Shabbos than most American Jews find it to observe the Shabbos.

"When an American Jew observes the *Shabbos*, even if only partially, he has to make a conscious, deliberate effort. He lives in a society where *Shabbos* has become Saturday. As you yourself said—business goes on as usual—indeed more so than usual.

"Having to work on *Shabbos*, the American Jew can easily reason himself out of any degree of Sabbath observance. You know the psychological sop—he doesn't want to be a hypocrite. When such a Jew builds synagogues, as he is doing today as never before, comes to *shul*, to a late Friday night service—ah, there is Jewish loyalty!

"Where Jewish education is concerned, much the same is true. In Vilna if a Jew had no learning, he was considered socially undesirable. He was looked down upon by the community. Jewish learning was thus quite crucial to living. In America, a Jew can be quite successful, quite acceptable—even the head of Jewish communal organizations—without Jewish learning. On the contrary, acquiring a Jewish education takes time and effort which might otherwise be used to further secular study which is quite indispensable.

"When, therefore, the American Jew, living in an environment which places a small premium on Jewish learning, which claims for itself the best hours of the child's school day—when he builds Hebrew schools as he is doing today all over the country at great personal sacrifice—that is Jewish loyalty. *B'dorotav*—even in his generation he is faithful to his tradition."

Turning now to the "*sholile hagolah*," the negators of the diaspora, Resh Lakish might say to them:

"God forbid that the American Jewish community should disappear—not only for America's sake but also for Israel's sake! For many, many years Israel will need the moral and material support of the American Jew. Israel will also need the cultural and spiritual stimulation of the diaspora. Israel will be more intensely creative if there is an export market in America for its cultural products.

"Historically, your fears seem to be quite groundless too. The fact is that Judaism has existed outside of Israel even when

78

there was a Jewish state. Marvin Lowenthal, the Jewish historian, points out in the latest "Zionist Quarterly," that between the re-establishment of the ancient Jewish state in Ezra's time until the destruction of the Temple in the year 70 C.E., there existed a Jewish state more or less self-governing, and fairly prosperous, to which any Jew dwelling in a foreign land could return. Yet we find that after a lapse of six centuries in which to come back, nearly three quarters of world Jewry lived in the diaspora, outside the Jewish state. . . . All of them were virtually free to return but didn't. Nor did their life seem sterile.

"Historically, therefore, there is every reason to believe that a free state of Israel and diaspora Jewry can co-exist. Moreover some of the greatest creations of the Jewish spirit were born in the diaspora. Ezekiel prophesied in Babylon; the Gemarra was created there. Rashi lived in France, the Tosefists in Spain and Germany, the super-commentators in Poland and Russia. And perhaps most significantly, the Golden Age of Spanish Jewry— the age of Yehuda Halevi, of Maimonides, of Ibn Gabirol—came after Jews had been in Spain for centuries. Judaism actually became stronger, not weaker, the deeper it sank its roots into Spanish soil.

"No! dear brothers, ours is not the last generation of Judaism in America. Any announcement of our death is as in the case of Mark Twain, grossly exaggerated."

So runs the debate. For myself, dear friends, I am prepared to believe that the process of diminishing Jewish loyalties in America has already been arrested and that Judaism is even now on the ascendency.

I do not think that Dr. Louis Finkelstein was altogether indulging in wishful thinking when he was quoted in the recent "Time," article as having said that: "Within 25 years, the vast majority of the five million Jews in this country will have returned to their faith and will be keeping the Sabbath." Dr. Finkelstein then cited the case of one of his friends, a very successful industrialist whose son is amazing him by turning into a brilliant Jewish theologian. He cited another instance of a 16 year old boy, who can step into his father's chain of retail stores but is determined to go to the Seminary and prepare himself for the rabbinate.

Is there a rabbi today who cannot point to such instances in his own community? Time was, when we would point to an unaffiliated, indifferent Jew and say: "You see this irreligious Jew. His father was a scholar, a *talmid chachom*." Today we point to a devoted synagogue worker and say: "You see this Jewish dynamo, his father cannot even read Hebrew."

Only recently, on a Sabbath morning, one of our very fine boys, sitting beside me on the pulpit seemed to be unusually nervous—even for a Bar Mitzvah boy. Trying to reassure him, I whispered to him: "David, you have nothing to worry about. You know the entire *Sidra* which you are reading from the Torah almost by heart. And you certainly know your *Haftorah*. Your *b'rachot* you knew three years ago. You're going to enjoy the service. Stop shaking."

In all seriousness, David turned to me and whispered: "Rabbi, I'm not worried about my part. I'm worried about the two *b'rachot* my father has to say."

Knowing David's father as I do, I can tell you the boy had every reason to worry. But the marvelous thing about that father is that he has devoted ten sacrificial years to building our synagogue and school.

Recently, a wave of indignation swept the Jewish community when several Jews, prominent in the entertainment world, made their scheduled public appearances on our High Holy Days. To be sure there were other Jews in public life who put their loyalties to their people's sacred days first. But the protest was naturally over those who did not.

Now what was significant in the incident, was not that the insensitive ones performed but rather that their performance evoked loud protest. I doubt whether there was such a protest over similar offenses two or three decades ago. Those were the days when on the East Side of New York anti-religious Jews would schedule Yom Kippur Balls on *Kol Nidre* night as close as possible

80

to the synagogue. And if their music succeeded in drowning out the synagogue service, then their evening was a howling success.

Commenting upon the incident of this year, the National Jewish Post said editorially: "In another decade, the Jewish stars of stage and screen and air waves will all almost naturally refrain from taking part in presentations on all important Jewish holidays." Ten years ago no one would have dared to make such a prediction. Nor would anyone have dared to predict ten years ago that a man named Will Herberg would this year have published a book called, "Judaism and Modern Man." At that time Will Herberg was one of the brilliant young intellectuals of the Socialist movement, quite distant from anything Jewish. Today Will Herberg has brought his gifted mind, and sensitive soul, to the altar of Judaism and has penned this book which the late Milton Steinberg called, "the book of the generation on the Jewish religion."

There are many more hopeful incidents that we could marshal, which buttress our faith in the future of American Judaism. But, I'm afraid I might draw too optimistic a picture and be among those whom Jeremiah castigated "for healing the breach of my people lightly." The rabbi should be the last to proclaim, "all's well," when, in fact, so much remains to be done.

But these random examples, and more that could be cited, are great omens of what we might become, of the great spiritual potential which is ours.

In the well known play "Green Pastures," Noah turns to God and says: "I ain't much, O Lord, but I'se all I got." Were I to write the Almighty's answer to that I would have Him answer Noah: "Noah you're plenty! You'se all you've got."

A well known *chasid*, Reb Zisha, used to say that in the world to come he was not afraid of being called before the Heavenly Throne and being asked. "Zisha, why weren't you like Moses?" He could answer quite honestly that he never had the capacities of a Moses. But he feared greatly that he might be asked: "Zisha why didn't you turn out to be Zisha? Why weren't you as great as you could have been?"

We American Jews will never have to answer before the bar of Jewish history why we were not Vilna Jews. We didn't live in Vilna. Times have changed. The environment has changed. But we ought to be vitally concerned about being asked: "Why didn't you become the American Jews you could have become?"

Admittedly it is more difficult to observe today than it used to be. But are we observing all that we can observe? Are we multiplying excuses when we should be doubling our efforts?

Granted that there are many obstacles in the way of a Jewish education. But there are also unprecedented opportunities. Are we pointing to the obstacles when we should be exploiting the opportunities?

True it is more difficult for us to attend services in the contemporary world than it was for our grandfathers in the pale of settlement. But never was a regular spiritual retreat more necessary than in the nervous and tense society in which we live. Are we visiting the synagogue as often as we must or at least as frequently as we can?

These, dear friends, are the questions that will be put to us. Let us so use the vast possibilities which are ours that a Resh Lakish in the Jewish tomorrow will be able to say of us:

"They were truly righteous in their generation." Amen.

REFUSING TO BE COMFORTED

An attitude of acceptance towards life is one of the crucial qualities for mature living. Nevertheless, there are many vital areas of our lives where we must refuse to resign ourselves to things as they are. Three such areas are reflected in three prayers which are part of the Rosh Hashanah liturgy.

Preached on Rosh Hashanah, 1953

10

Refusing to Be Comforted

SOME years ago there appeared an anthology entitled, "I Believe." It contained the personal creeds and convictions of some of the most prominent citizens of the world. One of these was the renowned American novelist Pearl Buck. In setting forth her philosophy she said that "the primary attitude towards life must be acceptance," and that this acceptance of life is the most significant act of the human mind.

I start at this point today, because during this season when we pray for life, we each list in our own hearts the things we should like the New Year to bring us and our loved ones. We are all sufficiently mature, however, to know that for many of us those prayers will not be answered. Life is never served à'*la carte*—not for too long, anyway. So that among the things we should pray for, it seems to me, is the power to accept whatever our portion, with courage and fortitude.

Acceptance is, as Pearl Buck indicated, one of the crucial qualities for grown-up living. We have to be able to accept economic losses. Most of us can remember the disastrous financial crash of 1929. The disaster was not, primarily, that people lost fortunes, but that many could not accept these losses and go on. So many committed suicide that it was being said with morbid humor that when a man checked into a hotel the clerk would ask him whether he wanted a room "for sleeping or for jumping."

We desperately need the power of acceptance when we, or those we love, sustain a loss of health or become handicapped. We live in a tension-filled society where it is not uncommon for a man in his prime to become physically handicapped by an ailment. At

85

such a time he has to be able to resign himself to more limited activity, a more deliberate pace of living and to go on with a handicap. (May I add, parenthetically, that all of us are really handicapped in one way or another, for Emerson was correct in observing: "There is a crack in everything God made.")

We need the power of acceptance, most urgently, when we sustain the loss of a loved one. How tempting and how human it is to be filled with despair over our possibilities of ever leading a meaningful existence again. Or we can become overwhelmed by self-pity, which has accurately been labeled as "a passport to insanity." Therefore, Judaism teaches that the kriyah, the cutting of the garment in the presence of death, be performed standing upright. Thus, it urges us to accept the inevitable encounter with sorrow standing erect, determined to go on living heroically, equal to the heavy burden that has been placed upon us.

Important as it undeniably is to be able to accept things as they are, there are times when it is no less important to refuse to accept things as they are, when we must reject things as they are, refuse to resign oneself to the existing situation.

This thought is suggested in this morning's Haftorah. The prophet Jeremiah is addressing himself to the children of Israel, who are in exile in Babylon. He is trying to sustain their hope for eventual restoration to their homeland. He tells them that in Ramah, Rachel's burial place, a voice is heard weeping and lamenting. It is the voice of mother Rachel crying over the bitter destiny of her exiled children. And the prophet adds the striking phrase: "Meyanah l'hinachem—She refuses to be comforted." She refuses to resign herself to the thought of permanent exile. She refuses to accept the fact of her children's eternal homelessness.

You can offer any explanation you wish for the miracle of reborn Israel. For myself, I am quite willing to sum it up in these two Hebrew words: "Meyanah l'hinachem." Our people refused to be comforted over exile. Other peoples before them and after them were driven out of their homeland. They shrugged their shoulders in an attitude of despair and proceeded to accept their new circumstances. The Jew alone refused to accept his new situation as permanent. Seventy-nine consecutive generations refused to be comforted. They fasted and wept on *Tisha b'Av*, and in a hundred other ways reminded themselves regularly of their resolve to return. That resolve became a fact in our time because they refused to accept things as they were.

This, of course, is true of every noteworthy human achievement. Trace back any worthwhile discovery or invention far enough, whether in medicine or in technology or in any field of human endeavor, and you will find its origin in the heart of a man who was disturbed and refused to be comforted, refused to accept things as they were.

George Bernard Shaw conveyed this thought with characteristic wit: "The reasonable man," he said, "adapts himself to the world. The unreasonable one persists in trying to adapt the world to himself. Therefore, all progress depends on the unreasonable man."

In this sense, dear friends, it is of vital importance that we become unreasonable. I submit that there are three decisive areas where we are too easily resigned, too prone to accept things as they are. In each of these, Judaism commands that we refuse to be comforted. These three areas are reflected in three brief prayers found at the beginning of our Rosh Hashanah *Amidah*, each of which is introduced by the word *uvchen*.

The first *uvchen* expresses the hope that all nations might form a single union—that there might indeed be a genuine United Nations.

I know that to express this hope today is to sound exceedingly naive or in some quarters to be guilty of disloyalty to a peculiar brand of Americanism. We have had wars of all temperatures—hot, cold and luke-warm. We are separated by curtains, divided by ideologies, rent apart by suspicion and hatred. East is east and west is west and never the twain shall meet—except perhaps on the atomic battlefield which shall blanket and fragmentize the globe.

Well, I say, that we ought not to accept that state of discord and enmity as final. We must refuse to accept a picture of mankind which dooms us and our children to annihilation or the threat of it.

In spite of all its weaknesses and short-comings, the United Nations represents the best hope on earth. It has made important forward strides in feeding the hungry and conquering disease. In Korea it has taken collective and effective action against aggression for the first time in human history. It has provided a forum from which opposing nations could address each other even if what they said has not always been complimentary.

The voices of reaction in our country have tried to undermine our faith in the United Nations. But, before we despair of it, let us remember that Isaiah and Micah spoke of a United Nations 2600 years ago. We Jews have been praying for it for millenia. But the organization is only six years old. Let us be patient with it and strengthen it in every way we can. Conceivably, we may not maintain peace with it, but we shall most certainly forfeit peace without it. In a world which has become a neighborhood, we need desperately to become a political brotherhood. In a world which has grown smaller, we must become bigger.

The tinsmith who constructed and installed the ballot box which the Security Council uses at Lake Success, put in it a scribbled note on which he had written a humble prayer. He asked God to be with every member of the United Nations and that their efforts bring peace to a troubled humanity. That humble tinsmith bespoke the prayers of decent people everywhere.

One of America's foremost citizens, Adlai Stevenson, just returned from a trip around the world. There was compelling wisdom in his words: "The door to the conference room is the door to peace. Let it never be said that America was reluctant to enter."

Let us refuse to be reconciled to a tension-torn world until we have expended every available effort to fulfill the first *uvchen*—"Let all nations form a single community to do Thy will with a perfect heart."

The second *uvchen* asks: "*Tayn kavod l'amecha*—Grant honor to Thy people." It expresses our prayer for the restoration of dignity to the Jew, a sense of self-esteem and self-respect.

Where our spiritual life as Jews is concerned, we are too prone to accept things as they are. The cancerous growth of Jewish ignorance which is daily eating away the vital tissues of Jewish life in America; the progressive dejudaization of our homes and the resultant inroads of divorce; the devitalization of our lives through the absence of Jewish moral and ethical values; the impoverishment of our weekly routine because it is uninspired by worship, unelevated by ritual; the growing incidence of Jewish names among those who break the laws of society; the evident lowering of our spiritual standards of living—we behold all this, and we say with resignation: "What can you expect? We live in an environment which is predominantly non-Jewish. We have to adapt ourselves to new circumstances. We must learn to march to the tune of different drummers."

Dear friends, we are too easily comforted! We should refuse to accept this lamentable state of spiritual affairs as normal or inescapable The fact of the matter is that Conservative Judaism refused to accept the progressive deterioration of Judaism in America as inevitable. And it has taken steps, successful steps, to return kavod to our people.

Among many achievements of our movement none is more inspiring to me than our summer Ramah Camps. (Another voice is heard in Ramah—refusing to be comforted.)

Whenever I feel the need to reassure myself about the enormous potentialities for a vibrant, creative Jewish life in this blessed land, I arrange to spend some time at Camp Ramah in the Poconos. It is a sight for tired souls. Hundreds of our children spend eight delightful weeks there every summer living by the rhythm of Jewish tradition, marking its Sabbaths, praying its prayers, singing its songs, speaking its language, tapping its sources, dramatizing its history, absorbing its values, becoming its hope. In an atmosphere saturated with the beauty of nature blended with the glories of "the tents of Jacob," our children joyfully discover for themselves the wealth and the challenge of their proud heritage. From there they return to their homes and their communities, living dynamos of dedicated spiritual energy.

What we are doing through our Ramah camps is perhaps our most dramatic accomplishment, but it is by no means our sole achievement. Through our intensified emphasis on adult education, on Sabbath observance, on Leaders' Training Fellowships, on youth work, on raising standards of synagogue life—through all these, and a host of other purposeful programs, we are proclaiming our faith in the rich future which awaits us on the American scene. We are announcing, too, that we refuse to be reconciled to our contemporary impoverished state of Jewish affairs as long as we have not exhausted our utmost resources to fulfill the prayer—"Grant honor to Thy people."

The last uvchen embodies the hope that we may soon see the day "when wickedness shall vanish like smoke." If we want to see wickedness disappear in the world, I suppose that we ought to begin with the wickedness within ourselves.

This task is more easily undertaken than accomplished. We are not overly prone to own up to the fact that we ourselves are part of the world's problem. When in rare moments we do make the frank admission that we are making our personal contribution to the wickedness of our society, we are too likely to accept ourselves as we are and to despair of our ability to change ourselves.

A few months ago a young man was in my study. His recently launched ship of matrimony was floundering on the rocks of discord and conflict. In fact, his mate had already abandoned ship. In describing the situation, he was careful to apportion the blame equally—50% was his wife's fault and 50% was the fault of his mother-in-law. When he was all through I asked him whether he thought that any portion of the blame for what had happened belonged with him. "Well," he said, reluctantly, "I guess so. I do have a habit of nagging."

"Well, why do you nag?" I asked.

He answered, "That's my nature. I can't help myself."

Judaism teaches us that we can change ourselves. We can struggle against the malice, the envy, the pettiness, the selfishness, the greed within us and triumph. That is the meaning of these days. Man's pre-eminence over the beast is that he alone can be better tomorrow. We need not be forever enchained by what we

90

have been. Our past need not be, forever, the cemetery in which our noble intentions must be interred stillborn. The Greek word for man is "anthropos," which means literally, "the upward-looking one." Man cannot only look upward, he can lift himself upward.

Luther Burbank, the genius of plant breeding, was moved by the belief that "every weed is a potential flower." The message of this day to us is that every man and woman is a potential saint.

After the tragic sinking of the Titanic, two pictures appeared in one of our newspapers. The first showed the ship with an open gash ripped into its side, listing helplessly, about to sink. The picture bore the caption: "The weakness of man; the supremacy of nature."

The other picture showed the passengers stepping back to give the one remaining place in the lifeboat to a woman with her baby in her arms. Underneath this picture were the words: "The weakness of nature; the supremacy of man."

Yes, we can triumph over nature, even our own. We ought, therefore, refuse to accept ourselves as we are until we have persistently done our best to make the wickedness within ourselves vanish like smoke.

For, herein, dear friends, is the key to it all. Unless we change ourselves, the world will not change, and certainly the Jewish world will not change. The last *uvchen* is the key to the others. That is why an ancient sage prayed so wisely when he asked: "Lord, change and make this a better world and begin with me." His sentiments were echoed by a modern poet who put this salient truth in these words:

> "Your task . . . to build a better world," God said.
> I answered, "How . . . ?
> This world is such a large vast place,
> So complicated now,
> And I so small and useless am.
> There's nothing I can do."
> But God in all His wisdom said,
> "Just build a better you."

It is noteworthy that our opening text from Jeremiah, which pictures mother Rachel weeping disconsolately and refusing to accept comfort, goes on to tell us that Rachel does receive a magnificent promise from God: "Refrain thy voice from weeping and thine eyes from tears, for thy work shall be rewarded. . . . Thy sons shall return to their own borders. There is hope for thy future." By refusing to accept superficial comfort, by refusing to reconcile herself to a situation which cries out for redress and which can in fact be redeemed, Rachel is promised the higher comfort—the ultimate end to the exile and a glorious homecoming for her children.

As long as we refuse to accept as final a divided humanity, a dejudaized Jewish community and our own unredeemed lives and we translate that dissatisfaction into an incessant struggle against these evils, then can we, too, hope to hear the reassuring promise of God: "There is hope for thy future."

Our theme can be summed up in the humble words of the man who prayed: "Dear God, grant us the serenity to accept the things we cannot change, the courage to change the things we can change, and the wisdom to know one from the other." Amen.

INVISIBLE LOSSES

In drawing up our moral balance sheets, we are very prone to
overlook invisible losses. Yet such losses can lead to spiritual
bankruptcy. Morally speaking, how solvent are we?

Preached on Yom Kippur, 1949

11

Invisible Losses

TAKING inventory, is an annual fiscal procedure which is familiar to every business man. Centuries before this became an established commercial practice, the Jew had developed the discipline of taking moral inventory. To some extent, he was prone to perform this task daily but on one special day of the year he did nothing else. This has remained the central meaning and the primary function of Yom Kippur—the supreme moment of *cheshbon hanefesh*, the day of days for taking stock of our souls.

There are, to be sure, some obvious differences between the two types of inventory. In the realm of finance others can, and often do, draw up our inventory ledgers for us. In the moral realm each man is his own accountant for he alone knows his true credits and debits.

There is another and more subtle difference. Business profits and losses are normally quite simple to compute for they are each entered neatly in red or black. Quite otherwise is the situation in the moral domain where our gains and setbacks defy easy computation and where, in addition, the entire calculation may be thrown out of balance because of our failure to take into our reckoning invisible losses.

In the section in the Talmud that deals with civil damages, there is laid down the unanimous legal principle that *hezek nikar shme hezek*—visible damage is considered a real loss. If A inflicts such damage upon B, B may sue for and be awarded compensation. The Talmud then raises the question: What if the damage inflicted by A upon B is *hezek she'eno nikar*—an invisible loss—is it still considered a real loss? If, for example, A does not destroy

B's grain but simply renders it ritually unfit to be eaten, may B sue A for damages in this instance? On this point there is disagreement between the Talmudic authorities. One opinion holds that an invisible loss is still considered a real loss for which compensation may be demanded. The contrary opinion contends that an invisible loss is not considered a compensable loss. In the Talmud this controversy remains unresolved. Both opinions are recorded for posterity.

This legal dispute seems quite remote from the area of our active concern. We are neither lawyers nor judges and I suppose that we are quite content to permit the professional minds to grapple with such intricacies of law. And yet, I submit, that in a very profound sense, quite apart from its legal implications, this controversy goes on within us all the time. Let us consider some telling examples.

When we have lost a loved one, there is no doubt that *sh'me hezek*—the visible loss is adjudged a real loss. There is weeping, there is mourning, there are condolences, there is *Kaddish*, there are *Yahrzeits* and there are, as we see today, Memorial Services. Yes, when we have lost a loved one all agree that we have sustained a real loss. But when we have lost the ability to love, the ability to pour forth affection, kindness and thoughtfulness, is this invisible loss, also a loss? Do we as much as recite a silent *Kaddish* for the capacity to love when it departs? Indeed, are we altogether aware of its passing?

When a man loses his wealth, all agree *sh'me hezek*—he has sustained a real loss. But when through greed or envy or the sole preoccupation with the amassing of more wealth, a man loses the ability to enjoy his wealth, is this invisible loss also a loss?

When the human heart goes bad all agree that *sh'me hezek*—a real loss has been suffered. The victim is hospitalized, confined to prolonged immobility. There is an outpouring of solicitude and concern. The man's pace of living is severely restricted. But when the heart turns sour and fills our souls with bitterness and our minds with malice is this invisible loss also a loss?

When we have lost a beautiful thing, all agree that *sh'me*

96

hezek. But when through disuse or improper cultivation we lose our appreciation for the beautiful is this invisible loss also a loss?

Should a physician suffer the loss of his practice, that would, indeed, be universally considered a real loss. But what if he loses sight of the humanitarian ideals that prompted him to join the ranks of the healers, would that loss be considered a real loss?

When hundreds of synagogues were destroyed in Europe all Jews mourned and felt personally impoverished. There was no doubt but that these visible losses were considered genuine losses. But, when through estrangement and absence, we lose our love for and our attachment to the synagogue are we quite as ready to admit that *sh'me hezek*—this invisible loss is also a loss?

Our Torah reading this morning began with a reference to the death of Nadav and Avihu, the two sons of Aaron. In seeking out the sins for which they were punished the later sages variously attributed to them moral depravity, excessive jealousy and unworthy ambitions. And most significantly the sages say of their death that it was "*srefat n'shama v'guf kayam.*" "Only their souls were consumed, their bodies remained unimpaired." Theirs was not a visible loss—only an invisible one. The humanity in them was destroyed, and that is equated by the sages with death itself. Perhaps, then, our sages are here confirming a moral verdict which they render more explicitly elsewhere. "The wicked even in life are considered dead." Thus, it would seem that while in the realm of civil damages Jewish tradition records divergence of opinion as to whether invisible losses are considered losses, in the moral realm our sages are agreed that invisible losses are also losses. Indeed, precisely because they are invisible they are so dangerous.

How ready are we to accept the moral verdict of our sages? Perhaps the classic believer that in the moral realm invisible losses are no losses, was Oscar Wilde's "Dorian Gray." We will recall that when Dorian Gray is but a young man, an artist, Basil Hallward, paints his portrait which reflects not only his striking physical handsomeness but also his inner spiritual beauty. When Dorian sees the portrait, he begins to cry. "How tragic, it is" he says, "that while I shall be growing old, and feeble, the portrait will remain forever young and handsome. How wonderful it would be if the reverse were true, if the portrait would grow old while I remained ever young and handsome." Even as he uttered his strange request it was granted.

Unfortunately, however, Dorian had not asked for enough. For while he was so disturbed about the physical beauty that he would lose, he was not at all concerned with his moral stature that might deteriorate. Dorian, like so many of us, was too preoccupied with the thought of visible losses, to give any heed to the invisible ones.

And so Dorian soon sets out in search of uninhibited self-gratification. He becomes, cruel, ruthless, merciless. He becomes so self-centered that he brutally crushes all who block his path. All the while his physical beauty and youth remain undiminished.

Soon, however, Dorian begins to notice that his portrait is changing. Hard lines begin to form about the mouth. A cruel glint appears in the eyes. The hands appear red and blood-stained. And so Dorian conceals the haunting portrait in the attic where it will not disturb him and where no one else will see it either. Somewhat uneasily, Dorian resumes his path of moral disintegration. Outwardly he is still the handsome youth but his invisible losses keep mounting. His integrity, his honesty, his humanity are all destroyed. Finally, when Dorian's moral decay has been completed, when he kills the artist who painted the picture, he rushes to the attic to view his portrait. He is shocked by what he sees. The youthful beauty has been displaced by frightening ugliness. His invisible losses have here left their deep visible scars. In a frantic effort to obliterate the terrifying reminder of his staggering invisible losses, Dorian plunges towards the portrait with a dagger to destroy it. He succeeds only in killing himself.

When his dead body is discovered, it is the body of a ghastly looking old man and smiling down upon him is the handsome portrait of youthful Dorian Gray. So, self-betrayed, Dorian had lived his life on the premise that *hezek she'eno nikar lav sh'me hezek,* but his ultimate self-destruction gave the shattering lie to his tragic self-delusion. A subtitle to Oscar Wilde's "Picture of Dorian Gray," might very well read: "Invisible Losses Are the Greatest of All."

Now, Oscar Wilde was quite far from being a religious man but because ultimately all truth must converge his parable did point up a profound religious principle. If Dorian Gray appears too exaggerated to be real, it is only because in wishing to make his point, Oscar Wilde stated it as bluntly and as forcefully as he could. But the more we learn about the workings of the human personality, the more impressed do we become with the tremendous negative role played by our invisible losses.

In recent years the field of medicine has been quietly undergoing a revolution which has found expression in a new dimension in medical thinking summed up in the phrase "psychosomatic medicine." If I understand them aright, medical men are now teaching that there is a genuine inter-action and inter-relationship between the human psyche, the human mind and the human body. Many a physical ailment, including such varied afflictions as paralysis, asthma and kidney trouble can often be traced not to any organic deterioration but to an emotional disturbance. A repressed sense of guilt, a deeply offended conscience, indeed, any severe invisible loss inflicted upon our emotional reserve, can wreak vengeance upon the body in terribly real and visible ways. Thus, men of science are today joining the moralists and the religionists in underscoring the heavy price we pay for our invisible losses.

The D.P. (displaced person) in Europe is at long last, thanks to the State of Israel, quickly disappearing. Here in America, however, our society is shot through with D.P.'s. Distressed persons, depressed persons, distracted persons, distraught persons, disturbed persons. Hence, the pre-occupation of Hollywood with psychological studies, superficial as they unfortunately too often are. Hence, also, the unusually rapid appearance and rise to popularity of such books as Peace of Mind, How to Stop Worrying and Start Living, Guide to Confident Living and Peace of Soul. Without being altogether aware of it, too many Americans are desperately groping to make good their invisible losses. They have no peace of mind, they are frightfully worried, they do not live confidently, their souls are at sea. The D.P. is still very much in evidence here and precisely in a land where material comforts abound and visible physical gains are most impressive.

Not very long ago there appeared an article in one of our national magazines entitled: "Our Most Important Shortage." In it the author said in part: "Physically and intellectually we are equipped as no other generation. . . . With enough of almost everything what we have too little of is the personal practice of an action-producing belief in Almighty God. . . . Our forebears who had too little of many things had more of that. . . .

"We have not found peace within ourselves. We have not been able to establish it among the nations. . . . Unless we are willing to prepare for a new Dark Age, we must soon acknowledge that good as we may think we are, we are not good enough to get along without the God our forebears found indispensable."

Thus, from all sides, we hear mounting evidence in support of an ancient principle of our faith. Invisible moral losses are at the very heart of the distress that afflicts human beings. No moral inventory which fails to reckon with them can yield any reliable figure. Any therapeutic measures which are not addressed to them are doomed in advance to failure.

We are told that he who weeps when he reads the story of Nadav and Avihu, the two sons of Aaron, and the peculiar death that overtook them, will win forgiveness for his sins. This statement is hardly intelligible on the surface, for Nadav and Avihu did very little to merit our respect let alone our tears. But there is a deeper meaning to this statement of our sages. What they are saying in fact is this. The tragedy of Nadav and Avihu, the tragedy of s'refat n'shama v'guf kayam—the deteriorated soul in the well-preserved body—was by no means an isolated historical tragedy. It is an ever-recurrent tragedy. In varying degrees it strikes at every human life. Only he can hope to escape it who sees in the tale of Nadav and Avihu so true a mirror of his own personal struggle that he is moved to tears. Only he can hope to check his invisible losses who honestly and sadly recognizes, to some degree, a reflection of himself in Nadav and Avihu.

On this Yom Kippur day before the Yizkor service when we ponder our visible losses let us also give serious thought to our invisible losses. Many of us have lost loved ones through death. How many more have lost loved ones through thoughtlessness, selfishness or stubbornness? How many families are being destroyed by conflict and friction? We remember the lament of the Italian mother in the film, "The House of Strangers." She sees her wealthy banking family being torn apart by dissension and conflict and she cries out: "Once upon a time when we lived behind the barber-shop we were poor but we were rich because we had love. But now that we are rich we are poor because there is hate. Ours is a house of strangers." How many of us are converting our homes into a House of Strangers?

How many of us are trying to purchase comfort at the cost of conscience? How many of us are trying to reach the pinnacle of financial success irrespective of the moral cost? How many of us are so concerned with our standard of living that we do not pay any heed to our way of living? How many of us are so concerned with accumulating the goods of life that we lose sight of the good life?

Ultimately there is very little we can do about controlling our visible losses. Loved ones are taken from us in spite of our most intense love and protection. Fortunes crumble in spite of wisdom. But in the realm of invisible losses, here, it is we alone who determine "who shall live and who shall die," who shall live grandly and who shall die in life?

For that, dear friends, is the meaning of the conclusion to the Untaneh Tokef prayer. "Penitence, prayer and charity avert the severe decree." Obviously these cannot keep us from physical death. Even the penitent, the prayerful and the charitable must die. Death is no respecter of virtue. But penitence prayer and charity do keep us from spiritual death, from deteriorated souls in preserved bodies.

On this day, then, let us each face wisely the choice offered us in the Bible. "Behold I set before you this day life and death. . . . And thou shalt choose life."

JUDAISM—FOR WHOM?

This question is too often given the wrong answer. For whose sake, indeed, should we be Jews? When we learn to answer this question properly, our lives can be transformed.

Preached on Kol Nidre, 1955

12

Judaism - for Whom?

ONE of the dominant motifs of the High Holy Day season is "*t'shuvah*—penitence" or, more literally, "returning"—in a moral sense. The ten day period from Rosh Hashanah to Yom Kippur is called "the ten days of penitence" and the keynote is sounded in the plea of the prophet Hosea which we will hear on *Shabbat*: "Return O Israel unto the Lord your God for thou hast stumbled in thine iniquity." These days sound a spiritual recall summoning us back to God, back to our heritage and back to our synagogue.

We who have answered the historic summons of our faith and have returned to this House of God, have probably done so for a variety of reasons, some of which may not altogether coincide with the reasons the prophet Hosea had in mind.

Sidney Lanier accurately reflected the religious temperament of our times when he said: "We live in a world of half faith and half doubt. Standing at the temple doors, head in and heart out." This is true of the larger society in which we live and it seems to be especially true of the Jewish world. Very often these lines come back to disturb me as I think of our spiritual household and its members. Even when we are within the synagogue, it frequently seems to me that many of us are only partially here, we're not entirely committed, we're not quite convinced of why we are here. We seem indeed to be "standing at the temple doors head in and heart out."

Let us stop today to consider a question which goes to the very heart of our Jewish living. This Judaism and Jewish life with which we are identified and affiliated, which we support and profess, for whose sake do we do so? Judaism for whom?

One answer that is frequently implied, in so much that we say and do, is that we live our Judaism for the Christians. If this statement sounds paradoxical, as indeed it is, let us pause to examine it briefly and we will find out what a disquieting amount of truth it contains.

Where Jewish education is concerned we are often indebted to Christians for the enrollment of a Jewish child in our Hebrew schools. From time to time a mother explains as she comes to enroll her child that she lives in a gentile neighborhood where all the children go to their Sunday School regularly. Her son is envious and wishes to do likewise. She is, therefore, bringing him to our Religious School. Another parent is aware that her child's gentile friends or teachers frequently ask questions concerning Jewish holidays and practices. She does not want her child to be embarrassed by ignorance. Hence the child is brought to the school in the hope that we will convert him into a walking Jewish information bureau. Credit our Christian neighbors with important assists in bringing these children to Judaism.

Once we leave the domain of the synagogue and venture forth into the maze of Jewish organizational life in America, the sensitivity to non-Jewish thought and opinion becomes even more pronounced. Only here it is not the understanding and well-meaning Christian who is reckoned with. Here it is the bigot who unconsciously largely molds the policies of Jewish organizations and provides a major stimulant to membership. The preoccupation with combating anti-Semitism at the expense of worth-while and creative Jewish activities is frequently pathetic and sometimes neurotic. The over-emphasis upon anti-Semitism has, too often, distorted our conception of a healthy Jewish life and has, instead, focused our energies upon this unhealthy obsession.

There is a story in a recent novel, "The Hunter's Horn," which underscores the folly and the danger of such an obsession. A Kentucky farmer became possessed with the task of hunting down a big red fox who had been marauding and killing chickens all over the countryside and who was therefore called King Devil. King Devil proved quite adept at escaping all the traps our good farmer set for him. But each failure only strengthened the farmer's resolve to capture him. And so he bought some very fine fox-hunting hounds at great cost and kept them at a burdensome expense. He fed them with the very best foods he could get. They had milk while his wife and children began to go hungry. Even the money realized from the sale of eggs the farmer used to buy food for the hounds. In his preoccupation with trapping King Devil, the farmer scarcely noticed his fences falling into ruins, his farm stock and soil wither, his garden and land deteriorate. In the end, the farmer not only did not catch King Devil but he also lost his home in the vain battle.

What a striking commentary we find in this story on the futility of so much we characterize as Jewish life today. We have been so obsessed with hunting the King Devil of anti-Semitism we have neglected the fences and meadows of Jewish life. We have lavished so much energy and money upon this vain pursuit that we have had little left with which to build a dynamic Jewish life. We have been so concerned about correcting the attitude of the non-Jew towards the Jew, that we have bothered too little with correcting the attitude of the Jew towards Judaism. Jewish life lived preponderantly for the non-Jew has been as unrewarding as it is undignified.

Another popular answer to the question "Judaism for whom?" often appears to be "Judaism for the children."

So many of us have come to look upon Judaism as a child's religion and the synagogue as a Kiddie Shop whose garments come only in juvenile sizes. The Bible is meaningful—for the children. Jewish rituals and ceremonies are appealing—to the children. Belief in God, decency and compassion are worthwhile—for the children. Jewish fellowship and comradeship are vital—for the children. Synagogue attendance is rewarding—for the children. We seem to be taking literally the biblical command: "And the children of Israel shall keep the Sabbath."

Judaism has of course always placed tremendous emphasis upon educating and indoctrinating the children. "And thou shalt teach them diligently unto thy children," was not permitted to remain only a biblical command. It was incorporated into the daily morning and evening services of the Jew. It was woven into the very fabric of his life. But the major underlying assumption was that the child would become a man and it wished to prepare him for reverent, humane and dedicated adult living. Today, however, much of our concern with our children carries with it the implication that as they grow older they will shed their religious practices and attitudes even as they discard their childhood clothes or their baby teeth. Thus, many of our people see nothing contradictory in absenting themselves from services even on the High Holy Days while they ask us to inculcate love and respect for Judaism in their children.

But can the synagogue hope to succeed in this mission when in the undisguised judgment of the parents this ancient and wise religion has nothing vital to say to them, when in effect they equate its age with senility? Our children, who are more perceptive than we usually think, can be excused if they ask themselves: "Can a religion suffering from second childhood have anything of value to say to us?"

A third answer to the question "Judaism for Whom?" often seems to be "Judaism for the departed."

At *Yizkor* time on Yom Kippur our synagogue attendance will suddenly show a remarkable and quite sudden expansion. The influx will be caused by the proponents of the philosophy of Judaism for the dead. The synagogue and its faith becomes meaningful to them only insofar as it affords them an opportunity to memorialize their departed.

The vitality and appeal of that type of Judaism can be only too well imagined. A Judaism for the dead is in fact a dead Judaism. Indeed, where only that is left of Judaism even that little soon departs.

No, dear friends, we cannot live our Judaism for our Christian neighbors or for our children or for our deceased. To be sure, each of these does play a legitimate role in our thinking; and in pleading for the creation of this synagogue, I have, in fact, frequently reckoned with them. I have tried to show how a beautiful synagogue will serve to raise our group standing and enhance our dignity in the general community. I have urged the creation of a school and synagogue as a means of transmitting the accumulated spiritual wealth of the ages to our children. And I have, from time to time, pointed out that the synagogue is the link which binds the generations one unto the other. But all these motivations for Judaism are derivative and secondary. For, basically, if Judaism is to have vitality and power, the primary answer to the question "Judaism for whom?" must be *Judaism for ourselves!*

For let us not delude ourselves. A Judaism that is devoid of meaning to us cannot inspire respect among our Christian neighbors. A Judaism unworthy of our loyalties cannot elicit devotion from our children. A Judaism that has itself become lifeless cannot even serve as a means of honoring the dead. It is only a Judaism which is throbbing and alive in us that can be transmitted to others and link the generations to each other.

In the Book of Genesis, there is an important verse which strongly suggests this very thought. God says to Abraham: "I shall establish my covenant between Me and thee, and between your children after thee throughout the generations for an everlasting covenant."

The sequence of the phrases in this verse is most significant. Note that the Almighty says—Abraham, this covenant must begin between Me and you. It is only if this covenant means something vital to you will it become also a binding agreement for your descendants. I make this covenant with your children, "after thee." And after it means something to them can it be a covenant, a binding power, a cohesive force "throughout the generations." After the Jewish generations have been linked together by the covenant, does it become a *"Brit Olam."* This phrase may properly be translated not only as "an everlasting covenant" but as "a covenant for the world."

It is we, ourselves, who must first enter into a covenant with God; it is we who must return to our ancestral faith and home—

only then do we have a right to expect that our children will do likewise. If we ourselves become a link, the chain of the generations remains unbroken.

How tragically wasteful it is, dear friends, to squander the accumulated spiritual treasures of our faith! We need them so desperately for ourselves. For it is we, ourselves, who in a world of uncertainty and insecurity must be able to feel with the Psalmist—"The Lord is my light and my salvation. Whom shall I fear?"

It is we who, in a world where sorrow is inevitable, must be able to affirm: "Yea, though I walk through the valley of the shadow of death I shall fear no evil for Thou art with me."

It is we who, in our struggles and strivings, must be able to proclaim: "He is at my right hand, I shall not stumble."

In a world which tends to reduce human existence to the jungle level of each man for himself and let the devil take the hindmost, it is we ourselves who must hear reiterated the divine summons: "Justice, justice shalt thou pursue."

In a world of selfish and arrogant strutting it is we who must hear the prophet's exhortation: "to love mercy and to walk humbly with our God."

In a world deafened by the clamor of material things it is we ourselves who must be reminded that "man doth not live by bread alone."

In a society which tends towards monotony and boredom it is we who need to hear the sweet poetry of Jewish ritual and ceremonial practice—"which if man shall do, he shall live by them."

In a world shot through with pessimism and fear of the morrow, it is we who need the fortifying faith that where there's an honest will, God finds the way.

One of the foremost psychiatrists of our time said recently: "Speaking as a student of psycho-therapy, . . . I am convinced that religion is the most valuable and potent influence for producing that harmony and peace of mind and that confidence of soul needed to bring health and power to this nervous generation."

"Return O Israel unto the Lord Thy God." Let us go back home. Back to the synagogue—our spiritual home. There our fathers and mothers found warmth, direction, confidence. There they gained the strength and faith which are the pre-requisites for integrated dignified living. Let us go home for our own sakes. There will be no mystical or magical transformation in us, but gradually the very atmosphere of the synagogue will bring us back on steady ground. Physically, as well as emotionally, our visits home will bring us strength. Our chaotically free lives will become integrated, purposeful. We will find some of that harmony and peace of mind which our generation is vainly seeking in best-sellers. Spiritual health, like physical health, comes not from reading but from exercise—spiritual exercise.

Come home O Israel. Come home and be at rest. Come home and be enriched. You'll be glad you came back.

"Return us O Lord unto Thee and we shall return, renew our days as of old." Amen.

FORGOTTEN MEN

Each of us is a bundle of many selves. Some of these we are too prone to forget. On the Day of Remembrance, they too ask to be remembered.

Preached on Rosh Hashanah, 1947

13

Forgotten Men

ONE of the names by which Rosh Hashanah is designated in our tradition is *Yom Hazikaron*—the Day of Remembrance. As we usually understand this phrase, *Yom Hazikaron* refers to God's remembrance of us, His creatures. Throughout the High Holy Day liturgy a recurrent motif is the prayer that God will remember us unto life.

I am sometimes also aware that the *Yom Hazikaron* is rapidly assuming another significance quite at variance with its original meaning. Instead of being a day when God remembers us, it is becoming one of the two or three lone days out of 365 when we pause to remember God.

But there is still a third interpretation of *Yom Hazikaron* that I should like to set before you this morning, an interpretation which I feel is at the very heart of this day, the very essence of its meaning and message.

President Roosevelt awakened the sympathy of this entire nation to the underprivileged among us when he spoke of "the forgotten man." Our hearts were aroused by the image of a neglected segment of our population whose needs, hungers and yearning were disregarded by their fellow Americans.

Today I should like to see in the *Yom Hazikaron* a charge to each of us to remember, also, other forgotten men—the many forgotten men within each of us, whom we neglect and disregard so persistently throughout the year.

In referring to ourselves, we each say "myself" as though we were a unified, single self. Psychology has taught us however, that in reality we are each a bundle of many selves all rolled together. Man is like a big bus with many little egos inside jostling each other. The rabbis of old grasped a measure of this truth when they spoke of the *yetzer hatov* and the *yetzer hara*—the good inclination and the evil inclination within each of us. But even this dichotomy was an over-simplification of the complex mechanism that the human being actually is. Each of us is a composite of multiple selves, often conflicting selves, each pleading for expression and recognition.

> "Within my earthly temple, there's a crowd;
> There's one of us that's humble, one that's proud
> There's one that's broken-hearted for his sins
> And one who, unrepentant, sits and grins.
> There's one who loves his neighbor as himself;
> And one who cares for naught but fame and pelf.
> From much corroding care I should be free,
> If once I could decide which one is me."

We know of course which self we should like to decide to be but the sad truth about most of us is that our nobler selves, our better selves, our higher selves, are somehow more easily forgotten during the rest of the year. They are our personal forgotten men.

Consider in the first place how often we forget the generous self within us. The selfish slogan which, too often, shapes most of our actions is, "What's in it for me?" We expect immediate dividends of personal return from every deed, from every solicited action. "And why not?" whispers our selfish selves, "self-preservation is the first law of life." And as the devil has been known to quote the scriptures for his own purposes, our selfish self can even quote the great Hillel, who said, "*Im en ani li mi li*—If I am not for myself, who will be for me?" In the army the saying went, "I'm taking care of No. 1."

But there is the more generous self within us too. In every worthy situation which demands that we give of our time, energy or substance, it pleads that we ask not, "What's in it for me?" but rather "What is there in me that I can give to it?" It reminds

112

us that while self-preservation is the first law of life, the crucial question is which self should we preserve, our selfish self, or our generous self. It reminds us, too, that Hillel, who said "If I am not for myself, who will be for me," did not stop there but went on immediately to add, "*u-ch'she-ani l'atzmi ma ani*—and if I am for myself alone, what am I?"

All of us are familiar with the promptings of our generous selves. It says to us: "A synagogue is being built in your community, go help build it. Do not shut your door and your heart while you hope that the few loyal synagogue workers will be so overburdened that they will not be able to contact you personally. Your brethren in Palestine need your support in their struggle to build our national home—do not withhold it. Distressed Jewry looks pleadingly to you, do not pretend not to hear."

The generous self within us reminds us that, "Thou shalt love thy neighbor as thyself," is not merely a Sunday School maxim, but an indispensable principle of living. It asks us to be generous also in word and thought, to follow the admonition of our sages to "Judge each man on a scale of merit."

The generous man within us is one of our forgotten men. Here is one man that this day of remembrance bids us to remember.

There is another self within us that we commonly forget, our aspiring self, the self which commands us to grow in spirit and character. It counsels us against measuring progress in terms of financial attainment, but rather in terms of heightened sensitivities, broadened horizons, deepened sympathies.

Our aspiring self pleads against our exclusive pre-occupation with activities which profit us neither morally, emotionally, intellectually or spiritually. It asks us not to kill time for time is the very stuff of life. It urges us to use it creatively and wisely.

A book which has enjoyed great success in our time has been concerned with "How to Win Friends and Influence People." I suspect that the basic reason for the popularity of the book is to be found in the widespread desire among us to get others to

113

do what we want. That seems to be a major impetus to making friends. Our aspiring self counsels that we try to make friends not only with our contemporaries but also with the great spirits of the past and that we permit our lives to be influenced by them.

The aspiring self also reminds us, as a philosopher once said, "We are not born human beings; we are candidates for humanity." To achieve that status we must constantly grow and move forward, we must not permit moral and mental cesspools of stagnation to develop within us. We must constantly permit new life giving streams to flow through us. In the words of Longfellow, "We must act in such a way that each tomorrow finds us further than today."

The aspiring man within us is another of our forgotten men. Here is another man that this day of remembrance bids us to remember.

The third self within us that we commonly forget is our religious self. At the end of the nineteenth century, it was quite fashionable to call oneself an atheist. Scientists had dethroned God and Colonel Robert Ingersoll was daring Him publicly to strike him dead if He existed. Today, atheism is somewhat out of style, but the conventional pose is to appear irreligious. So many of us hasten to announce, lest the rabbi or anyone else misinterpret our zeal for the synagogue, that we are not religious. I maintain that an irreligious man was not yet born. Man is by nature a worshipping creature. In his infancy and early childhood he worships heroes. As modern man grows up he frequently deludes himself into believing that he has outgrown the need to believe and the capacity to worship. The truth of the matter is that when he stops believing in God, he starts to worship something else and calls that God. Judaism calls that idolatry, but a god each man has. Sometimes gold becomes god, the bank becomes a temple, the banker the high priest, the bankbook the Bible. Sometimes as in recent history, the state, the Fuehrer, or science becomes God. Man is a worshipping animal and each man has his shrine.

Where religion is concerned there are two types of hypocrites.

114

There is first the man who proclaims his piety but his performance, alas, falls distressingly short of his professions. Then there
is the self-proclaimed irreligionist, the "I-am-not-religious—but
. . ." person who often practices and most frequently believes far
more than he is ready to admit.

Rare, indeed, is the individual among us who can stand atop
a tall mountain over-looking the wondrous hills, the enchanting
landscape, the soft shades of nature's coat of many colors and
not be filled with a reverence of a psalmist who proclaimed, "the
Heavens declare the Glory of God, and the firmament testifies
to the work of His hands." "A man," said Lincoln, "may declare
himself an atheist when he looks down upon earth, but no man
can fail to believe in God when he looks up at the heavens." How
many among us can see our child recover from an illness and not
feel a deep sense of gratitude to the benevolent Power that heals?
How many of us can face a crisis without feeling impelled to call
upon a sustaining Power greater than ourselves? How many of
us have not felt, from time to time, with the poet, a presence
that disturbs us with the joy of elevated thoughts?

So that, when a man announces that he is not religious, I
do not take that to mean that his religious self has been destroyed. He is announcing that he has tried to forget his religious self by failing to cultivate it. Rosh Hashanah bids us to
remember the religious man we are so prone to forget.

The last self within us that we frequently forget is our Jewish
self—das pintele yid. That this self is not dead within us is eloquently attested by our presence here today. It is this self which
is inflamed whenever the name of the Jew is dishonored, whenever the person of the Jew is outraged. But this Jewish self is
not only sensitive to humiliation and hurt, it has more positive
demands. It wishes that we inform ourselves and our children of
the glories of our history, the nobility of our heritage. It is
ashamed, not of itself, but of its own ignorance of itself. It is
uncomfortable at the thought that it has become alienated from
the source of its life, its destiny and its purpose.

Our Jewish self asks that we adorn our homes with a mezuzah

115

and Jewish works of art, that we fill our shelves with books of Jewish content and inspiration, that we hallow our homes with the *Shabbat*, the candles and the dietary laws, that we do not permit the House of God to remain only God's private home, but that we make it our home too. It forbids us to act in a way which may degrade the name Jew and thereby cause *chilul Hashem*. It urges that we stop being Jews at heart and become Jews with all our hearts, with all our souls and with all our might.

The Jewish man is another forgotten man within us. Here is another man, Rosh Hashanah bids us remember.

Many a tombstone bears the inscription, "Gone, but not forgotten." Many of our better selves could be labeled, "Forgotten, but not gone." Because they are not gone, but merely forgotten, Rosh Hashanah is hopeful of forcing them to the level of consciousness and infusing them with the breath of life.

Alexander the Great, we are told, sitting in judgment on one of his subjects, found him guilty and sentenced him to death. "I appeal," said the man. "Appeal? To whom?" asked Alexander, "I am the highest authority." "Your Majesty," said the condemned man, "I appeal from Alexander the Small to Alexander the Great." Rosh Hashanah likewise appeals from the small men within us to the great men within us. This is the basic meaning of this day.

On this day of remembrance let us be mindful that we are not alone in praying, "Remember us to life." The forgotten men within us also utter those words. Let us resolve to face the New Year in a spirit of remembrance, to make of our lives an "amen" to those prayers whose fulfillment depends upon us alone. If we remember the forgotten men within—our generous self, our aspiring self, our religious self, and our Jewish self—then, indeed, shall we ourselves have been remembered to life, to a life which will never be forgotten.

REMEMBERING AND FORGETTING

We cannot remember everything. Nor should we. What kind of memories shall we seek to perpetuate? Which shall we strive to erase?

Preached on Yom Kippur, 1951

14

Remembering and Forgetting

AT Yizkor time we become gratefully aware of the blessing of that God-given human power called memory. A significant portion of the Rosh Hashanah service including the Torah and Haftorah readings for the first day underscores the theme that God remembers. Today before the memorial services it is we who do the remembering. Through memory we confer immortality upon the souls of dear ones. They continue to abide among us. They walk with us again. They teach us, they inspire us, they comfort us. At Yizkor time we understand what the poet Whittier meant when he wrote: "Grant but memory to us and we can lose nothing by death."

And memory does more than give us back the past. It also gives us the present. Without memory the business of living becomes a chaotic enterprise. Were we unable to remember from one moment to the next, the world would become a labyrinth in which it would be impossible for us to find our way. We could acquire no useful habits. We would be as helpless as infants. Our days, to be coherent, must be strung together by the golden thread of memory.

It is impossible of course on the conscious level to remember everything. Even the finest memories can retain only a small fragment of their experiences. Nor indeed is it desirable that we remember everything. On the contrary, important as is the power to remember, no less important is the power to forget. Life as we know it would be unlivable if we were not blessed with the gift of forgetfulness. If we had to live each day burdened with the crushing weight of all our past griefs and bereavements, if we could not banish from our minds our accumulated failures, frustrations and fears, if the wounds we suffer on life's battlefield were always raw and gaping—then life would be an intolerable curse.

There is a beautiful *Midrash* which underscores this truth. A Jewish legend tells us that when the Almighty finished creating the world and He was about to release it, He suddenly realized that He had forgotten an indispensable ingredient without which life could not endure. God had, as it were, forgotten to include *Shikchah*—the power to forget. So He called back the world and blessed it with *Shikchah* then He was satisfied that it was ready for human habitation.

Many of us frequently complain that our powers of memory are not as strong as we should like them to be. Without realizing it, however, many of us suffer from the fact that our powers of forgetting are not as keen as they should be. Here's the way a poet put it:

> "This world would be for us a happier place
> And there would be less of regretting
> If we would remember to practice with grace
> The very fine art of forgetting."

Now, just as we cannot remember everything so is it impossible if we are healthy in mind to forget everything. Only the amnesia victim has complete *Shikchah*. The alcoholic and the dope addict can obtain temporary forgetfulness but the price they pay for that temporary release from memory is tremendously exhorbitant, not only financially but also in health and human dignity.

If, then, we can neither remember everything nor forget everything, what shall we remember and what shall we forget?

The answer it seems to me is to make our memories selective and discriminating so that we remember those things which are likely to make us better people and nobler characters and we forget those things which are bound to shrink us in stature and weaken our characters. We ought to exercise the same selective care in furnishing our memories as we do in furnishing our homes.

Of course it will be objected that memory is largely automatic. As a rule memory does not select and reject. It does not discriminate. It is not like a sieve which separates the wheat from the chaff. It is more like a barrel which catches whatever is poured into it.

That however is only part of the truth. Actually memory never operates independently. Working alongside of it is judgment and judgment guides memory.

The celebrated philosopher Immanuel Kant was once jolted by the discovery that his servant Lampe, whom he had trusted implicitly for long years, had in fact been robbing him steadily and systematically. Kant had no choice but to dismiss him despite his heavy dependence on him. Understandably, Kant did miss him terribly. In the philosopher's journal we read the echo of his sadness: "Remember to forget Lampe." Kant was enlisting his judgment in the service of his memory to help it reject Lampe.

A massive illustration of this truth came at a crucial juncture in American history. In 1941 the judgment of the American people decided that whatever else we permitted to grow dim in our collective memory, one thing that we would not forget was Pearl Harbor. On billboards, over the radio, at mass meetings, the slogan "Remember Pearl Harbor" was hammered home into our memories. And our determined prosecution of the war effort to its successful conclusion is evidence that the American people did "Remember Pearl Harbor." Our intense preoccupation today with strengthening our world-wide defenses at a staggering cost so that we never again be caught unprepared is evidence that we still "Remember Pearl Harbor." Here the judgment of America guided its memory.

This truth has operated dynamically in Jewish history too. The great Lawgiver, Moses, decided at the dawn of our people's history that whatever else the Jewish people forgot, there was one memory they must always keep alive. "And thou shalt remember that thou wast a slave in Egypt." No less than fifty times is this

121

command in one form or another repeated in the Torah. Through the annual *Seder* the Jew has vividly re-enacted the experience of Egypt. It is, therefore, no accident that the Jew has always been in the forefront of those who fight for the oppressed, the down-trodden, the underdog. To this very day, the Jew has remembered that he was a slave in Egypt because the collective judgment of the Jewish people determined that Egypt was not to be forgotten.

And if, today, Israel is an independent Jewish state it is also because the judgment of our people decreed 2500 years ago: "If I forget Thee, O Jerusalem, may my right hand be forgotten." Other nations before and since suffered exile too. But for them exile meant death and disappearance. The Jew not only survived, he lived to rebuild and reconstitute his homeland. He accomplished this unprecedented historical feat because in a thousand ways he kept alive the memory of Zion. In his daily prayers, in his grace after meals, under the wedding canopy—in every conceivable way he remained faithful to his vow of eternal remembrance. Zion was not forgotten because in the judgment of our people its memory was to be kept eternally alive.

Thus, we see that judgment not only molds memory but that memory in turn molds behavior and character. This is true not only of groups and nations but also of individuals. We are what we remember. A keen student of human behavior, George Halifax, has correctly said: "Could we know what men are most apt to remember we might know what they are most apt to do."

What shall we remember and what shall we forget?

In the Bible we find Joseph facing this same memory problem in one of the most dramatic moments in his eventful life. The moment occurs when Joseph who had been sold by his brothers into slavery now finds these brothers before him. But now he has become the regent of Egypt and his brothers, driven by famine, appear before him for food. Joseph has them at his mercy. He can do with them as he wills. But what will he do? His problem is fundamentally one of memory. What should he remember?

He can remember how they maltreated him, cast him into

the pit where he might have been left to perish had not an Ishmaelite caravan fortuitously appeared, how they coldly traded him away as if he were no more than a piece of sheepskin or a measure of corn. Or he can remember how he the young Joseph had provoked them, how he had brought tales of malice about them back to his father, how he had taunted them with his dreams of his destined domination over them. He can either remember the wrong he suffered or the wrong he inflicted. He can either exact vengeance or make amends. Which experience shall he remember?

This problem is not easily solved. Instinctively, Joseph appears ready to exact vengeance. In a variety of subtle ways he torments his brothers, worries them and hurls accusations against them. All this, however, is but the prelude which leads up to the climax—the moment when Joseph reveals himself to his brothers. When that moment arrives Joseph emerges in heroic stature. He has chosen to forget his brothers' misconduct and to make amends for his own.

When he notices the fear that registers on their faces he tells them: "Be not angry with yourselves that you sold me here, for God sent me before you to be a preserver of life. It was not you but God who sent me here." He then goes on to assure them that he will make arrangments for them and their families to live in Egypt where he will provide for them all. In this way does Joseph solve his personal memory problem.

The beginning of the New Year 5712 is an excellent time for us to draw up our memory balance sheets. We neither can nor wish to carry into the New Year all the mental records of 5711. Nor can we or should we obliterate every trace of memory of the year just ended. We must carry some memory accounts forward and what we remember of 5711 will in large measure determine our actions in 5712. What therefore shall we try to leave behind? What shall we try to carry forward?

"Ma'ase avot siman libanim—the actions of the fathers are a guide to the children." Joseph's experience can be highly instructive. We must try to forget those things which if remembered

123

would bring out our unworthy traits. We must try to remember those things which if forgotten would suppress our nobler instincts.

Some among us during the past year permitted ties of family and friendship to be broken. There was an unpleasant scene, a heated exchange of words, an explosive moment. We chose to remember that moment while we forgot all the unnumbered pleasant moments of family loyalty and warmth of friendship. Would it not be much wiser now if we forgot the hurt and remembered only the love?

All of us during the past year have suffered wrongs and inflicted them. Too often we recall the instances when we were the victims; we forget those where we were the offenders. Were it not wiser to reverse our memory systems—consign the wrong suffered to oblivion and repair, where time yet permits, the wrong inflicted?

All too often we remember with bitterness the unfulfilled promises made to us but we calmly forget the pledge we made and did not honor, the resolve we made and did not keep, the word we gave and did not fulfill. Were it not better that we forgot the first and remember the second?

None among us has not been both benefactor and beneficiary during 5711. We have benefitted others to be sure but in more instances than we normally care to remember we have also reaped the harvest of another's kindness, another's generosity, another's sacrifice. If we enjoy the blessings of health, freedom, democracy, Judaism, it is because others have paid for these, our possessions, with their lives and their blood. Shall the little kindnesses we have shown make us haughty when there is so much that we have inherited which should make us profoundly grateful and humble?

Every day we see about us evidence of human pettiness, greed, self-centeredness and irreligion. But if we observe carefully we also see human nobility, generosity, self-surrender and genuine religious conviction and action. The cynic remembers only man's faults—that is why he remains a cynic. The righteous man remembers his brother's virtues. Which shall we choose to remember in 5712?

In the year just passed not a few among us have endured the anguish of final parting from a loved one. Parents and children, brothers and sisters, husbands and wives have tasted the bitterness of bereavement. They are now left with a choice of memories. They can either languish in pining as they dwell upon the death of their dear one or they can find inspiration and ennoblement as they contemplate the life of their beloved. They can either become bent under the burden of grief or be braced by a sense of gratitude. From their loss they can either distill an unending flow of tears or derive deepened sympathies, clearer vision, nobler strivings. Which shall be remembered in 5712—the loss or the love, the death or the life?

These questions each of us will have to answer for himself. In making our choice let us remember that we shall be what we remember. Our memories will mold our action and what others will remember of us will be determined by what we choose to remember.

I should like to close with a poem called "Old Year Memories," which sums up beautifully our thought for this Yizkor hour:

"Let us forget things that vexed and tried us,
    The worrying things that caused our souls to fret,
    The hopes that cherished long were still denied us—
Let us forget.

Let us forget the little slights that pained us,
    The greater wrongs that rankle sometimes yet,
    The pride with which some lofty one disdained us—
Let us forget.

But blessings manifold, past all deserving,
    Kind words and thoughtful deeds, a countless throng,
    The faults o'ercome, the rectitude unswerving,
Let us remember long.

125

Whatever things were good and true and gracious,
Whate'er of right has triumphed over wrong,
What love of God or man has rendered precious—
Let us remember long.

So, pondering well the lessons it has taught us
We tenderly may bid the year good-by,
Holding in memory the good it brought us,
Letting the evil die."

WHAT CAN WE PROVE BY YOU?

Our true objective as Synagogue Jews is not to build sanctuaries but to become sanctuaries. One of our most conspicuous
failures has stemmed from our refusal to face this truth. Franz
Rosenzweig's life points the way for us.

Preached on Kol Nidre, 1956

15

What Can We Prove by You?

SHORTLY before the holy days, I received a letter which stimulated my thinking about a problem which fully deserves our attention on this night of *Kol Nidre*, when we should be vitally concerned with the spiritual destiny of the American Jew. The letter was written by a woman who has chosen to remain outside the orbit of the synagogue but what she says is not without vital relevance for all of us who are within its walls.

Permit me to read a somewhat condensed version of her letter:

"For some years, and after considerable intellectual and spiritual probing, both my husband and I have felt most strongly that we are unable to accept the existence of a deity. Because of our lack of faith we find ourselves unable to become members of any social institution whose prime purpose is the worship of a God.

"We have a child, now five and a half years old, of highly developed intelligence. We have told our child our religious beliefs and have also told her that our beliefs are not a majority view. She has been introduced to a more than appropriate Christian indoctrination in the public school of our community. She accepts and fully believes in a God. She is eager to identify herself with her religious group and to be educated in its principles.

"We feel that the anti-religious bias we present to our child must be counteracted by an education in her religion so that in later years she may make an intelligent and satisfying decision concerning her affiliation. We feel further that the responsibility of such education should be accepted most willingly and sincerely by the Jewish synagogue, regardless of the parental beliefs.

129

"I do, most sincerely, hope that you will be able to accept our child in your school program and give her what her mind and spirit presently crave—a religious way of life."

After I had re-read the letter carefully, I telephoned our correspondent to tell her that the synagogue was fully prepared to accept the educational responsibility for her daughter, provided the parents were willing to assume the financial responsibility for that education. This portion of the conversation took a few minutes and was concluded quite amiably.

As I spoke to her I was looking at that portion of her letter where she had written:

"After considerable intellectual and spiritual probing both my husband and I have felt most strongly that we are unable to accept the existence of a deity."

Before concluding the conversation I was anxious to know just how considerable was this "intellectual and spiritual probing." And I asked her specifically if she had read any books about Judaism. No, she hadn't. Had she participated in any synagogue service? No, she hadn't. Had she heard any Jewish sermons? No, she hadn't. I expressed the hope to her that she would affiliate with a congregation and use the resources of the synagogue, its library, its adult education program, its services and sermons, to help her in her probing.

After I hung up the telephone, my heart was weeping silently over the spiritual tragedy of so many of our people. Of course, a Jew has a right to reject his Judaism but does not that very right impose a prior obligation to understand what it is he is rejecting?

As Jews we pride ourselves on the freedom of thought we allow within our ranks—a latitude few other religions permit. But do we have a right to confuse freedom of thought with freedom from thought?

I have no quarrel with the Jew who studies Judaism, informs himself of its beliefs and doctrines, and then says, "I am sorry, I cannot accept that!" I may regret his conclusions, but I cannot challenge his right to them. They were arrived at honestly.

But does a Jew have a right to dismiss cavalierly, to reject out of hand, vast resources of mind and spirit which numberless Jews developed and preserved with their very lives? Does this not represent the most wanton kind of wastefulness? Does the right to be different give us the right to be indifferent?

As these thoughts lay heavy on my heart, there came to mind the image of Franz Rosenzweig. Let me tell you about him.

The year is 1913. The place is a small orthodox synagogue in a little German city called Cassel. The Yom Kippur services are in progress. The Cantor has already proclaimed the traditional formula before *Kol Nidre*: "With Divine sanction, and with the sanction of this holy congregation, we declare it lawful to pray together with those who have transgressed." Little does anyone suspect, however, that the congregation today includes a young man of 27 on the verge of the ultimate transgression. He has come to take last leave of Judaism before he embraces Christianity.

Franz Rosenzweig's brilliant mind had been nurtured on a heavy diet of philosophy. Of his own faith he knew pathetically little. Small wonder that it had offered him such meager sustenance. The teacher whom he revered most deeply was a Christian. One day Rosenzweig confronted him with a question freighted with a sense of personal urgency. "What would you do," he asked him, "if all answers fail?" The professor answered with soft earnestness: "I would go to the nearest church, kneel and try to pray."

The impact of this answer upon the groping soul of the young man was profound. It crystalized into a fateful decision. He, too, would seek that same haven of secure refuge in the reassuring bosom of the church. Indeed, many Jews had already done so, frequently out of less pure motives. Many, like Heinrich Heine, had regarded the baptismal certificate as the ticket of admission to European society. Rosenzweig's integrity would not permit so sordid a spiritual transaction. He would turn to Christianity for the same rich rations which fed the inner hunger of his admired teacher.

But his systematic German mind laid down one condition. To become a Christian, he must arrive by way of Judaism. Was

131

that not the path followed by the founders of Christianity? Rosenzweig would enter the door of the church not as a pagan but through the exit of the synagogue. And in what place and time could the official leave—taking of his people and his faith be effected more fittingly than in the synagogue on the Day of Atonement?

This was the mood in which Franz Rosenzweig entered the humble synagogue in Cassel on Yom Kippur 1913.

We know what he heard in the synagogue that Yom Kippur day. He heard what you and I shall hear during the next twenty-four hours. He heard of a God who is near to all who call upon Him, to all who call upon Him in truth; a God who can be approached in honest confession by the humblest Jew without any human intermediary. He heard of the eternal compassion of God for the folly and weakness of man. In the *Haftorah* from Isaiah he heard the cry of God's messenger to undo the bands of the yoke, to let the oppressed go free, to deal bread to the hungry, to clothe the naked, to house the homeless. In the recitation of the moving story of the Jewish martyrs slaughtered for *kiddush hashem* by imperial Rome, he heard the agonized cries of the anonymous Jewish spiritual heroes of all ages who were vandalized but not vanquished. In the story of Jonah, he heard of God's profound concern for the non-Jewish city of Nineveh, even for its beasts and cattle. And when the shadows had fallen across the faces of the worshippers and the *Shofar* blast announced the end of the solemn day of fasting, Rosenzweig was still part of the congregation which rose to its feet and with one voice proclaimed the battle-slogan of the Jew: *Sh'ma Yisrael Adonai Elohenu Adonai echad.*

Soon thereafter it became apparent that that Yom Kippur day was indeed a day of conversion for Franz Rosenzweig. He converted to Judaism. What started out as a day of mean desertion was to become a day of momentous discovery.

Shortly thereafter he writes to a friend telling him that he has reversed his decision to become a Christian. "It no longer seems necessary to me and . . . no longer possible." In another letter he recognizes the meaning of the church to the world—namely, that no one can reach the Father except through the Christian redeemer. But, he says, "the situation is quite different for one who does not have to reach the Father because he is already with Him."

World War I found Rosenzweig in a German uniform. From the Macedonian trenches he would send postcards and letters to his mother daily and in them he would include some of the thoughts about his newly-discovered faith that were spilling over in him. In true motherly fashion, his mother treasured these cards and letters and when he shed the uniform, he was to use these notes for his great work, "The Star of Redemption," in which he sought to convey the vast richness of Judaism to a wavering generation. He organized and conducted an Academy for Jewish learning in Frankfort and thus exerted a personal, lasting influence upon hundreds of disciples who have carried his name and his influence to Israel and America.

In 1922 Rosenzweig was stricken by a crippling paralysis which was accompanied by almost incessant pain. His limbs soon were reduced to uselessness. His nerves betrayed their function. After a few years, he could not move his head nor utter a sound. But he relentlessly pursued his translation of the Bible, his commentaries upon the Jewish prayers and liturgy. When he was powerless to write, he would indicate letters one by one on an alphabet chart to form words. When death finally released him at forty-two it put to sleep a still vital, creative mind of a devout Jew.

Can you see why I thought of Franz Rosenzweig after my telephone conversation? If he could speak to my correspondent (and he could if she took the trouble to read his life's story in a Jewish Publication Society book published three years ago), he could be so helpful to her. He could take her and her husband by the hand and lead them back to the synagogue where they would find repose and serenity. He could help them heal the dangerous spiritual breach of a home religiously divided against itself. He could give them the Jewish indoctrination they need to counteract the Christian indoctrination their five and a half year old daughter is now, according to her mother, receiving in the public schools.

But, as you may surmise from my lengthy retelling of his life story, it is not of her alone I am thinking tonight. To all of us here, Franz Rosenzweig speaks a real challenge. For if those outside the synagogue have rejected Judaism too casually, we have accepted it too casually. There is not enough of a difference between them and ourselves. We have not made the effort to acquaint ourselves with Jewish history, its vocabulary, its literature, its teachings. We have grown too complacent to permit our ignorance of our heritage to disturb us. We have failed, also, to regard Judaism as a way of life which demands personal commitment in action not only on state occasions but every day of our lives.

Recently, I had the dubious privilege of spending a very long hour in the company of a man who had the distressing habit of repeating a rather popular expression. No matter what topic presented itself for discussion, he was ready with his pet comment: "You can't prove it by me." We ranged over many fields— politics, golf, juvenile delinquency, the weather—and with rare consistency our so-called conversationalist kept injecting, "You can't prove it by me."

Much later that night, long after the human record had been turned off, the monotonous refrain lingered on. I couldn't expel it from my mind. Suddenly, I realized that in this expression there is summed up the real weakness of Jewish religious life in America.

The sad truth is that there are too many things about Judaism that nobody could prove by the lives of Jews who belong to synagogues.

If someone were to ask: "Is *Shabbat*, the cornerstone of Judaism, really vital?" how many affiliated Jews would be compelled to answer, "You can't prove it by me?"

If someone were to ask: "Is prayer with the congregation at

regular intervals truly necessary?"—how many synagogue members would be compelled to answer, "You can't prove it by me?"

If someone were to ask: "Does a child's Jewish education really require a parent's personal example and constant active interest?"—how many synagogue Jews would be compelled to answer, "You can't prove it by me?"

If someone were to ask: "Does a Jewish home really give a special tone and quality to life?"—how many affiliated Jews would be compelled to answer, "You can't prove it by me?"

If someone were to ask: "Is it true that Judaism is both a way of looking at the world and a way of living in the world—in our shops, our offices, our factories?"—how many affiliated Jews would be compelled to answer, "You can't prove it by me?"

I submit, dear friends, that if there were more truths about Judaism that could be proved by those inside the synagogue, there would be fewer Jews outside it.

The significance of Franz Rosenzweig for us is that he said to the world: Judaism is of the utmost importance and you can prove it by me!

When our ancestors were commanded to build the first sanctuary in the wilderness, they were told that God's purpose was, "so that I might dwell among them." Our sages, with fine ethical sensitivity, noted that the Bible did not say, "so that I might dwell in the sanctuary," but rather "among them." The sanctuary was not meant to contain God but to radiate Him. The individual Jew was himself to become a sanctuary, a dwelling-place of the Divine.

We, at Temple Sinai, have mightily enhanced the physical and spiritual landscape of our community by erecting an impressive sanctuary worthy of the high purposes to which it is dedicated and the rich heritage it embodies. No one knows better than I the mountains of devotion, conscientious and sacrificial love that went into its creation. But all our efforts will be vitiated unless we realize that our true objective as Jews is not to build sanctuaries but to become sanctuaries, to reflect in our lives the glory of God and the grandeur of Judaism.

135

"Every Jew," said the Belzer Rabbi, "should so conduct himself that his sons will rejoice to say, as Jacob did: 'The God of my Father.' " Rabbi Leib Saras went further. He indicated that your responsibility and mine extends beyond those whose lives have flowed directly from our own. "The good man," he declared, "should himself be the Torah and people should be able to learn good conduct from observing him."

When Franz Rosenzweig re-embraced his ancestral faith, he did so with conviction and he followed it by commitment. Like him, may we translate our loyalty into concrete *mitzvot*, daily duties and acts of self-sanctification. May we so live that we may merit the tribute spoken of one of Browning's characters:

> "Through such souls alone
> God stooping shows sufficient of his light
> For us in the dark to rise by. And I rise."

Amen

WORDS

A popular expression tells us that "words are cheap." Our tradition has an entirely different estimate of their worth. How can we restore to words the value which they have lost in modern times?

16

Words

WE live at a time when the spoken word, like the American dollar, has greatly shrunk in value. Neither accomplishes as much as it used to. A variety of factors have contributed to the devaluation of words in contemporary life. In the United Nations, Russia's emissaries speak of the "People's Democracy" in Hungary which they most recently "liberated," a second time, by executing 2,000, imprisoning 45,000 and deporting 12,000 to that cradle of "democracy," the Soviet Union. Ibn Saud interrupts his slave dealings long enough to appear at Lake Success to give the world a lecture on human dignity and equality. Here at home, the "word merchants" are bombarding us three times during every 15 minute radio or television program, with paeans of praise and hymns of glory to their sponsor's toothpaste or deoderant. The message of these "Hidden Persuaders" is crucial. We can disregard it only at the risk of our popularity, our success or lonely Saturday nights.

And as far as conversation is concerned, the popular estimate of its worth is perhaps most trenchantly revealed in a gadget which I chanced upon in a novelty shop recently. It consists of an upper and lower set of real looking teeth joined together by a winding mechanism. After winding, the teeth beat together feverishly and produce the unedifying sound: "Yackety-Yack." All this, taken together, lies behind the oft-repeated verdict: "Words are cheap."

But what a steep price-hike words undergo as soon as we enter the synagogue on *Kol Nidre*. The very prayer which gives its name to this holy night—*Kol Nidre*—means "all vows" and deals with our repentance for vows, obligations and oaths we made and did not keep. Underlying this entire prayer which keynotes the most sacred day on our calendar is the recognition that the plighted word is sacred, that the broken word profanes and corrupts the soul. Words are *not* cheap, says *Kol Nidre*, they are immeasureably holy.

Nor is this theme permitted to fade from our liturgy once we have finished the *Kol Nidre*. Like a haunting refrain it keeps recurring throughout the spiritual symphony of the twenty-four hour fast. Consider only the *Al Chet*, the confessional, which is repeated in each of five services starting with *Mincha* this afternoon and ending with *Mincha* tomorrow. What prominence is explicitly given to the sanctity of words!

"For the sin which we have committed before Thee with utterance of the lips;
For the sin which we have committed before Thee in speech;
For the sin which we have committed before Thee by unclean lips;
        . . . by impure speech;
        . . . by denying and lying;
        . . . by scoffing;
        . . . by slander;
        . . . by idle gossip;
        . . . by tale bearing;
        . . . by swearing falsely;"

And, significantly, the entire confessional is followed directly in the silent devotion by the prayer which we repeat thrice daily —"O my God, guard my tongue from evil and my lips from speaking deceit."

No, says Yom Kippur to us. Words are not cheap. They are infinitely precious.

In our finest moments we know that the truth lies not with the cynical slogan of the times but with the timeless verdict of our tradition. A bride and groom under the canopy betting their lives on each other and summing up this fateful decision in a few words, do not believe that words are cheap. A young man being interviewed by a prospective employer for a position for which he has prepared himself over long hard years, does not believe that words are cheap. A lawyer pleading desperately for the life of his client does not believe that words are cheap. Children gathered around the bedside of a dying father who is leaving his last verbal legacy, do not believe that words are cheap. At such moments surely words become freighted with an urgency and a decisiveness which leave their permanent imprint upon human lives. At such critical junctures we accept the judgment of our tradition that "Life and death are in the power of the tongue."

But Judaism goes beyond these spectacular and dramatic moments. It tells us that at all times, in every circumstance, words are holy. For it is in this God-given power to speak, to utter syllables and to frame them into intelligible means of communication with other people that we have one of the truly distinguishing human traits which separates us from the beasts. In medieval Jewish philosophy, man is called "medaber," "the one who speaks," for it is this faculty which differentiates him from the rest of the animal kingdom as well as from the world of nature.

A few months ago, we marked at Temple Sinai the Bar Mitzvah of a deaf boy. Among other things, this experience brought me a deeper understanding of the affliction of those who are consigned to the world of silence. But there was one thing that was said to me by the woman who acted as the interpreter of the service to the predominantly deaf congregation which I simply could not absorb. She quoted Helen Keller to the effect that deafness is a greater affliction than blindness. It sounded incredible. Surely I thought if any normal person were confronted with the heavy necessity of choosing between these handicaps, he would prefer to be in silence than in darkness.

In the intervening months I have thought often of this remark of Helen Keller's and I think I now understand why she, who certainly should know, declared deafness to be the greater curse. Blindness isolates its victims from the world of things.

141

Deafness cuts a man off from people. A blind man sitting anywhere in this congregation tonite would feel part of the congregation. A deaf man would feel terribly alone. A blind man at a social gathering would be part of it. A deaf man without an interpreter would feel quite excluded. It is through words that we maintain our contact with each other. They are the bridges over which we are constantly moving into the lives of others. Words are sacred indeed.

What care should, therefore, be exercised in our manner of using words! Who does not know the fearful power of words! "A word fitly spoken," says the Bible, "is like apples of gold in settings of silver." Of course it is. And what of the word uttered in anger? How many families has it divided, how many friendships has it fractured, how many marriages has it soured?

Words heal grief and they open wounds, they lift us up and they crush us, they bolster our confidence and they rob us of our dignity. Used thoughtfully they can enhance our regard for another; used maliciously, they splinter reputations. Where speech is concerned there are far too many amateur photographers in circulation. How they love to take something negative, develop it in the dark room of their minds, enlarge it and then mount it for public display. Words, says a Yiddish proverb, should be weighed not counted.

And what of the words we should speak and do not? Thomas Carlyle's wife was a highly gifted person, one of the most clever women in England in her time. She loved her husband dearly and to the extent that he was capable of loving any woman, other than his mother, he loved her too. After her death, he read this entry in her diary: "Carlyle never praises me. If he says nothing I have to be content that things are all right." He had been living with a woman whose heart hungered and ached for years for a kind word of appreciation and praise—a word which this prolific writer of words had never brought himself to utter. Yes there is indeed perilous potency in words.

Words are more, too. They not only admit us into the lives of others. They are also mirrors of our own souls.

It would be, for example, a very instructive commentary on the progressive weakening of Judaism in our lives to concentrate on a few key words in the vocabulary of the American Jew.

Consider the *Shabbat* for one. Our grandparents never spoke of the Sabbath without putting the adjective holy before it. "The Holy Sabbath is coming," they would say. They prepared as extravagantly as they could for this royal guest. Its departure filled them with nostalgia and a yearning for its return the following week. Our parents dropped the adjective holy and referred to it simply as the Sabbath. For us, it has become the week-end. A very weak end indeed!

When a Jew of yesterday wanted to call attention to one of his blessings, he never did so without adding, "Blessed be the name of God." When we wish to mention our good fortune, we look for a piece of wood to knock on.

At this season of the year our forebears greeted one another with the traditional: "A good year." We wish each other: "A happy New Year." They emphasized the thought that life's central quest was for goodness, for uprightness. With us the accent falls on the pursuit of pleasure.

Even the way we refer to these days of Rosh Hashanah and Yom Kippur reveals a decisive difference in attitude between our ancestors and ourselves. We close our shops or absent ourselves from our businesses on account of the Jewish holidays. To them they were Jewish Holy Days, days of awe and trepidation. Now it may not seem to be a vital distinction but there is indeed a world of difference between a holiday and a holy day.

On holidays we run away from duties.
On holy days we face up to them.
On holidays we seek to let ourselves go.
On holy days we try to bring ourselves under control.
On holidays we try to empty our minds.
On holy days we attempt to replenish our spirits.
On holidays we reach out for the things we want.
On holy days we reach up for the things we need.
One brings a change of scene, the other a change of heart.

143

One pampers our bodies, the other nourishes and challenges our souls.

So then, whether we are observing the holy Sabbath or spending a week-end, thanking God for our blessings or frightening away evil spirits by knocking on wood, hoping and wishing for a good year or a happy year, observing holidays or holy days—speaks volumes about the kind of Jews we are.

And words reveal also the kind of human beings we are. Our words mirror our characters. Psychiatry has taught us among other things that there is no such thing as an "idle word." The most casual remark, the word spoken "off guard," often furnishes the expert with a vital clue to our inner selves. Even our slips of the tongue are not without significance. Our charity towards others, our estimate of ourselves are all mirrored in our language.

A piece I chanced upon recently points this up sharply:
"Isn't It Funny . . .

When the other fellow takes a long time to do something, he's slow,
But when I take a long time to do something, I'm thorough.
When the other fellow doesn't do it, he's too lazy,
But when I don't do it, I'm too busy.
When the other fellow goes ahead and does something without being told, he's over-stepping his bound,
But when I go ahead and do something without being told, that's initiative!
When the other fellow states his side of a question strongly, he's bull-headed,
But when I state my side of a question strongly, I'm being firm.
When the other fellow overlooks a few of the rules of etiquette, he's rude,
But when I skip a few of the rules, I'm original.
When the other fellow does something that pleases the boss, he's polishing the brass.
But when I do something that pleases the boss, that's cooperation.

144

When the other fellow gets ahead, he sure had the lucky
    breaks.
But when I manage to get ahead, Man!
Hard work did that!
Funny, isn't it—Or is it!"

Words are holy. They are bridges. They are powerful. They
are reflections of our souls and character.

And yet, after we have said all this, a lingering suspicion remains that the popular estimate that "words are cheap," is not
altogether devoid of truth. In Yiddish we say—der olum iz nit kine
golum. It is an untranslatable expression but in essence it proclaims that any proverb widely trumpeted contains at least some
gleam of insight, some kernel of truth. And so this one does in
fact. For all our emphasis upon the importance of words, the
popular slogan calls attention to the insufficiency of words. Words
are too often emptied of their meaning because they are not
supported by action, they are not accompanied by corresponding
deeds.

This truth helps us, I believe, to understand one of the sins
which I did not mention earlier when I listed all the sins of
words which are catalogued in the confessional. The list certainly
seemed quite adequate to cover all transgressions we commit in
speech. But then there is one more which is puzzling: "Al chet
shechatanu l'fanecha b'viduy peh—For the sin which we have
committed before Thee with the confession of our mouths."

The precise meaning of this sin is not too clear until we look
at it against the background of the expression "words are cheap."
That indeed seems to be sin we are repenting of, that we have
cheapened words, we have confessed great truths with our mouths
but we have not translated them into deeds. This is the sin of
lip service, words which become not a stimulus to action but a
substitute for them. It happens to be one of our most prevalent
sins too.

A recent survey revealed that some 95 to 98% of the American
people believe in God. It would seem that God never had it so
good as in America today. But in this same survey there was

another question which asked: "Would you say your religious beliefs have any effect on your practice in business or politics?" To this question a majority answered no. Their religious beliefs had no effect on their conduct in the decisive areas of everyday life. Religion has become respectable but irrelevant.

This points up one of the deep-rooted maladies of our time which is closely related to our widespread anxieties and emotional ailments. We are split spiritual personalities.

We swear allegiance to one set of principles and live by another.

We extol self-control and practice self-indulgence.

We proclaim brotherhood and are guilty of prejudice.

We applaud service and practice selfishness.

We laud character but strive to climb to the top at any cost.

We erect synagogues but our shrines are our places of business and recreation.

I read recently of a minister who preached so well and lived so badly that when he was in the pulpit everybody said he ought never to come out again, and when he was out of it everyone said he never ought to enter it again.

That preacher is actually a lot of us, suffering from a distressing cleavage between the truths we affirm and the values we live by. Our souls are the battlegrounds for civil wars and we are trying to live serene lives in houses divided against themselves.

This is the core of the spiritual problem of our times not only in our individual lives but also in our corporate life as citizens of a democracy. The desperate battle going on in America over integration, our State Department's acquiescence in discrimination against American Jews in Saudi Arabia are only some of the more conspicuous manifestations of the sin of lip service, confession of the mouth unrelated to corresponding deeds. I think it was Harold Laski who warned that "the surest way to bring about the destruction of a civilization is to allow the abyss to widen between the values men praise and the values they permit to operate." We can overlook this warning at our own peril.

Yom Kippur urges us to narrow the abyss between our professions and our practice, between our words and our deeds, to restore the value to the words we have cheapened. For unless we do, we shall never find life's most basic necessity.

The biographer of D. H. Lawrence made a profound observation which was prompted by his study of his bitterly disappointed subject and which goes to the very heart of this matter. "When a man is sure that all he wants is happiness," writes Middleton Murry, "then most grievously he deceives himself. All men desire happiness but they want something different, compared to which happiness is trivial, and in the absence of which happiness turns to dust and ashes in the mouth. There are many names for that which men need but the simplest is wholeness."

My very dear friends, on this holy night let us hear the summons to become whole people, to restore our battered integrity, to bridge the divide within ourselves, to restore the sanctity to our spoken words.

What beautiful words we shall speak during these next twenty-four hours. We shall give expression to remorse, we shall frame great resolves, we shall echo the undying hopes of the household of Israel. Let us clothe these words with high purpose by adorning them in the sacred garb of appropriate deeds.

As the prophet, whose words we read during the season of penitence, charges us—*k'chu imachem d'varim*—let us take these beautiful words with us. Let us not leave them behind in the synagogue but let them inspire our actions and direct our deeds. May the days to come bear impressive testimony that we consider words holy indeed. Amen.

DO A LITTLE MORE

Whether the alleged "religious revival" among us is genuine, is the subject of lively debate on the American Jewish scene. The ultimate verdict hinges upon our actions. What can we do to lend impetus to the revival of Judaism in our lives?

Preached on Kol Nidre, 1958

17

Do a Little More

YOM Kippur is the last and climactic day of the Ten Days of
Penitence. Its central theme is a call to T'shuvah. It sounds
a summons to retrace our steps back to the path from which, during the past year, we may have wandered. Its underlying assumption at all times was that during the course of the year the Jew
was prone to fall below the standards he had set for himself.
Yom Kippur, therefore, held up a familiar standard to which the
erring Jew could repair. It attempted to win him back to the
way of life from which he had temporarily strayed.

For many of us, this call to return is still valid. But, I am
acutely aware that there are also many among us, how many I
have no way of knowing, for whom a call to return has an empty
ring because they have never been more observant, more loyal,
more committed. If anything, they have been living more Jewishly in recent years than ever before in their lives. Many of us
who belong to this congregation are children of parents who never
belonged to any congregation. We are the parents who are giving
our children a measure of Jewish education our parents did not
give us. Many of our mothers, who are lighting the *Shabbat*
candles, do not have similar memories of their own childhood
to invoke. They are enrolled in a host of Jewish organizations to
which their parents never belonged. They support a myriad of
Jewish causes their parents never knew. When they pray: "Return us unto Thee, O Lord, and we shall return, renew our days
as of old," they are talking largely of olden days they never knew
in their own immediate experience. At best, these are days in
the dim recesses of Jewish history of which they have heard tell.

149

If, then, our lives are to know a deeper religious fervor, if we are to bring our own straying footsteps back to the Jewish way of life, the call to many of us tonight must be, not a call to return but, a summons to advance. "Speak unto the children of Israel and let them move forward."

That the American Jewish community has in recent years already taken some impressive forward strides is a demonstrable fact. I have already alluded to some of the evidence in our own lives. There are other significant phenomena. Our own experience in this community is by no means exceptional. In 1942 our problem was to fill a synagogue with a seating capacity of about 350. Since then more than a half dozen spacious synagogues have been erected within a two mile radius of Temple Sinai. On this day of Yom Kippur we shall be providing services for some 2500 men, women and children. And to our great distress, we turned away scores of families whom we could not accommodate.

A generation ago, the key word in the messages from synagogue pulpits across the land was "survival." We were literally struggling for our very lives as Jews. We were fighting a holding action, trying desperately to cling to some refuge against the combined onslaught of the anti-religious proletarian elements, the assimilationists and the self-hating Jews. Today the key word is "revival." We have moved from the defense to the offense. We are no longer content with not dying. Now we want our corporate life to be dynamic, creative and purposeful. The cry of the faithful of the 1930's *"lo amut*—I shall not die," has given way to the second half of that verse—*"ki echyeh*—I shall surely live."

This massive revolution in the spiritual psychology of the American Jew was neatly summed up by Maurice Samuel with characteristic insight and crispness. As one of the veterans of the Jewish lecture platform he has been addressing audiences from coast to coast for several decades. In a recent article he notes that there has been a telling change in the type of question he hears in the discussion period following his presentation. In years gone by, the most persistent question used to be: Why should I be a Jew? Today it is: How can I be a Jew? We are no longer tormented Hamlets endlessly soliloquizing to be or not to be a Jew. Today, we are looking for the substance of Jewish living, the vital ingredients with which to fill the container labeled "Jew."

And we have begun to find the ingredients. Our congregational schools are growing at a pace which simultaneously taxes and embarasses our teacher training seminaries. The Jewish Day School is spreading at an unprecedented rate and it is no longer the sole concern of Orthodox Judaism. There are already a host of Solomon Schechter Day Schools, fathered by the Conservative movement, and new ones are being added with encouraging frequency. Summer camps with meaningful Jewish cultural and religious programs are dotting many peaceful countrysides which hitherto were the exclusive preserve of camps teaching Indian lore and giving our children Indian summers. We already have four Ramah camps and if we had the trained staff, we could fill four more camps over night. Last summer we turned away one thousand would-be campers. On the cultural scene there is a constant flow of new books on Jewish subjects. Jewish music and art are progressively enriching more of our homes and lives.

Marcus Hansen, a sociologist who studied the behavior patterns of Scandinavian immigrants to America, pointed out that the children of immigrants usually tend to reject their parents' ethnic and religious behavior patterns. In their effort to adjust to new surroundings, the members of the second generation slough off everything which is foreign and hence likely to prove an obstacle to their integration. Their children however, the third generation, already quite secure in their Americanism, are receptive to their grandparents' religious patterns. Thus, said Hansen, it would seem that what the sons of immigrants wish to forget, the grandchildren wish to remember. Hansen's law, as it is known, appears as applicable to the descendants of the Jewish immigrant as to the descendants of the Scandinavian immigrant. Many a second generation Jew who hastily discarded his religious baggage in an effort to facilitate his entrance into the American mainstream, has lived to see his own children put forth heroic efforts to retrieve the abandoned parcels.

151

All this weighty testimony notwithstanding, there are some trained and respected observers of the Jewish scene who seriously question the genuineness of the alleged religious revival among us. They point, for example, to some comparative studies that have been made among Americans of the three major faiths. To the question: "Are you a member of a church or synagogue?" an affirmative answer was given by 87% of the Catholics, 73% of the Protestants but only 50% of the Jews. The question: "Have you attended religious services within the last twelve weeks?" was answered positively by 82% of the Catholics, 68% of the Protestants and only 44% of the Jews. There was a third revealing question: "How often do you read the Bible?" An answer of "never or hardly ever" was given by 32% of the Protestants, 56% of the Catholics and 65% of the Jews.

Disturbing as these comparative figures are, they do not by any means constitute the most telling arguments of those who question whether a meaningful revival is indeed sweeping through the spiritual household of American Israel. Their criticism is less a quantitative one than a qualitative one. It is not so much a question of how many Jews have returned to the synagogue but rather why they have returned and to what they have returned. Thus one astute and altogether sympathetic observer feels impelled to write: "The third generation in affirming Judaism is not being drawn by the pull of its historic faith, but is being propelled by the pressures of its contemporary environment. Rather than asserting a spiritual identity, it is conforming to a social situation. Here is no inner ferment, no creative quest, but only a new type of acquiescence." If we might transpose this thought into the terminology introduced by David Riesman in his sociological study, "The Lonely Crowd," we would say that the American Jew's return to Judaism has been "outer-directed" not "inner-directed." It was not set in motion by any genuine hunger of his heart or thirsting of his soul or searching of his mind. Its motive power was a desire to adapt to the prevailing American scheme in which every citizen feels impelled to join his own church, the avowed enemy of "atheistic communism." This is the least a respectable citizen can do as a member of "one nation, under God" whose chief of state is dutifully photographed every Sunday as he emerges from his house of worship.

Because our motivations for returning have been so largely superficial, our actions after returning have been so conspicuously sterile. The critics are not overly impressed by the splendor of our new synagogue structures. These they dismiss either as a manifestation of the "edifice complex" or as a reversion to the "stone age." We build synagogues and we use them primarily, for social purposes; we send our children to religious schools but make little or no effort to enlarge the pitifully meager Jewish knowledge we ourselves possess. Our Jewish consciousness comes perilously close to being a Jewish unconsciouness because we know that we are Jews but we have only the vaguest intimations of what Jewishness is.

There are few living Jews among us who have labored so earnestly and sacrificially in the vineyard of American Judaism as has Dr. Mordecai M. Kaplan. His sober words on this subject therefore merit particular attention. "The back to the Synagogue movement," he wrote, "is a movement with its back toward the synagogue and its front away from it."

Why do I rehearse the testimony of the critics on this Kol Nidre night? Is it to mock your efforts? God forbid that I should be guilty of such a sin. And if the sheep have gone astray is it not the shepherd who must answer?

I have summoned up only the voices of those critics who chastise us out of love, who believe in our future and who mean to rouse us out of our lethargy and apathy. They want us to convert a pale and anaemic revival into a vital and living rejuvenation. They challenge us, as this holy night is meant to challenge us, in the words of Ezekiel: "Make you a new heart and a new spirit for why shall you die, O house of Israel?"

What then shall we do to live?

We must re-think our relationship to Judaism. Needed is an overpowering desire to go beyond affiliation to commitment, to start thinking not only in terms of belonging but in terms of becoming. The decisive demonstration of what Judaism really means to us will be given in the arena of action. We will have to prove ourselves capable of one of the most difficult human achievements—a change in our pattern of living.

Professor Abraham Heschel has written the prescription for this transformation. It is the essence of simplicity. Speaking at our last Rabbinical Assembly convention he urged us to challenge every Jew: "Do as much as you can and then just a little more than you can. This is vital—a little more than you can."

Professor Heschel himself is a thoroughly observant Jew. But notice what he is asking of us. He is not asking us to become what he is. He is asking us to become more faithful than we now are.

A journey of a thousand miles begins with a single step. May I suggest some such steps that we can take.

The first step I would urge upon every one of us who has not yet taken it, is learn to read Hebrew. Learn to read Hebrew! The goal for Temple Sinai for 5719 is to make every man and woman a Hebrew reader. To help us realize this objective we will ask those of us who know how to read to volunteer to teach their fellow members who do not. We will organize intimate study groups which will meet throughout our community afternoons and evenings. If past experience is any guide, a pupil should master the rudiments of Hebrew reading in six lessons. Is there any reason for literate Jews to remain Hebraically illiterate?

The newspapers recently told of an elderly Irishman in Hackensack, New Jersey, who learned how to read Hebrew so that he might know the thrill of reading the Bible in Hebrew. Can we do less? For us, reading Hebrew is the key to worship, the door by which we enter into the living fellowship of Israel past and present. It is also indispensable for our future. "The Jews of America," said Solomon Schechter, "cannot live without English but they will not survive without Hebrew."

Here are some other steps we can take if we have not already taken them:

1. Attend at least one synagogue service, on the Sabbath or the week-day, during every week of the year.

2. Subscribe to and read at least one Jewish periodical a week and read at least one book of Jewish interest every two months.

3. Refrain from eating forbidden meats and sea food both inside and outside the home.

4. Refrain from performing all truly avoidable labors, commercial or domestic, on the Shabbat. For our men this means a soul-searching examination as to whether it is absolutely necessary to go to their places of employment. For our women this entails eliminating cooking, house cleaning, clothes washing on the *Shabbat*. For both this means avoiding shopping and smoking.

5. On the positive side, our women could resolve to usher in the *Shabbat* with that profoundly poetic and spiritual act, the lighting of the candles. Our men should learn and recite the *Kiddush* at the beginning of the Sabbath meal. Together every effort should be expended to make the Friday night meal a hallowed ritual on the weekly family calendar. No avoidable commitments should keep us from our family table.

6. Every meal in the home should begin with the *Motzi*, that simple blessing over the bread which restores us to our proper human dimensions and underscores, if only for a fleeting moment, our utter dependence upon the mercies of a gracious God. The main meal of the day should be followed by the abbreviated version of the grace after meals, preferably in Hebrew but at least in English.

7. Where our children are concerned we should strive to give them a maximum Jewish education for the maximum number of years.

8. We should seek out opportunities to attend worship services with them as often as possible throughout the year.

9. We should join at least one organization in addition to the synagogue which is committed to furthering Jewish life whether in America or in Israel.

10. Within those organizations our voices should be raised in behalf of richer Jewish content and deeper loyalty to Jewish values and sanctities.

These, then, are some ten steps in addition to learning to

read Hebrew that we can take. I put them forth with some apprehension. The few among us who are already observing more will protest that I am asking for too little. The many who are observing less will protest that I am asking for too much. Notwithstanding the anticipated objections from the right and left, I have ventured to list some basic acts of Jewish commitment because I believe a beginning has to be made to translate our vague religious sentiments into concrete acts, into *Mitzvot*. To those who are observing more I say in the words of the Haggadah "Kol hamarbeh hare zeh m'shubach—the more you do the more praiseworthy." I am not issuing a new "Shulchan Aruch," a new code of Jewish law for you. To those for whom these steps seem too demanding, I repeat the words of Prof. Heschel: "Do as much as you can and then a little more than you can." If we do something, that is better than doing nothing. If we do more, that is better than doing something.

What is important for all of us, is that we recognize the implications of our membership in Temple Sinai. What we are saying in effect is that Judaism is sacred, its survival in us and through us is a cherished objective, that we mean to project it into the unborn future. None of these implied affirmations have any validity apart from the specific impact Judaism makes upon our way of life, in the things we do, because we are Jews, and in the things we abstain from doing, because we are Jews.

What I am pleading for tonight is not alone that we bear testimony to the revival of Judaism in us, but that we permit Judaism to revive us, that it hallow our daily ground, impart a glow of spirit to our secularized lives and invest our momentary deeds with a dimension of the eternal. "Do as much as you can and then a little more than you can."

HUMILITY—A LOST VIRTUE

An effort to recapture a basic Jewish virtue in an age which puts little emphasis upon it. In what perspective must we look upon ourselves if we are to fulfill the injunction of Micah "to walk humbly?"

Preached on Shabbat Shmot, 1955

18

Humility — A Lost Virtue

A few months ago, a very prominent television personality discharged a singing member of his staff and gave as his reason: "He lost his humility." If the discharged star was somewhat devoid of humility before his dismissal, we have reason to fear that he has even less today, because this accusation and the resulting dismissal projected the young man into instantaneous prominence and financial success. The alleged loss of humility thus proved no real deterrent to our singer.

In many people's minds, there was some lingering confusion as to who was really deficient in humility—the accused or the accuser. Somehow, the virtue called "humility" is one which the possessor must carry without being too conscious of it. The moment a person becomes aware of his humility, he loses it. For then it is very tempting to say, as Gilbert and Sullivan's Mikado did: "You have no idea how poor an opinion I have of myself and how little I deserve it." The Chasidic Rebbe Mendele of Kotzk made the penetrating observation that of all the mitzvot in the Torah, the mitzvah of humility is the only one which does not require conscious intent. On the contrary, the presence of such self consciousness negates humility entirely.

You can understand my reluctance to deal with this theme. To call attention to a lack of humility is almost tantamount to convicting oneself of the same fault.

Moreover, ours is a society singularly incongenial to the flowering of humility. This is the age which has created the high-pressure publicity agent and promoted advertising into one of America's major industries. Neither of these developments was triggered by an excess of modesty. Indeed, if a sense of humility ever descended upon Madison Avenue, many a publicity and press agent would be stricken with total disability and we should probably never know again the touching musical tributes to soap suds or the heart-warming poems in praise of dog food.

In recommending a man for a job or an applicant for admission to a school, we are apt to call attention to his reliability, industry, integrity, intelligence. Rarely, if ever, would we think of including humility among his attractive qualities. For humility in our time is almost a lost virtue.

And yet, humility runs like a golden thread throughout the Jewish pattern of righteous living. Indeed, among the Chasidim, humility was regarded as the top rung on the ladder of perfection.

Consider, for example, the biblical profile of Moses. In many real ways, he is the central hero of the Jewish drama. It was he who planted in the heavy hearts of a down-trodden slave people the yearning to be free. It was he who led them triumphantly, in spite of themselves, out of Egypt. It was he who served as God's agent for the Revelation at Sinai. It was he, again, who led them for some forty years through the fierce and forbidding desert—a journey made more difficult by the nostalgic backward glances towards Egypt which the rabble rousers among the people were perpetually casting. There were so many noteworthy qualities of Moses that the Bible could have singled out for praise, and yet there is only one direct compliment which Scripture pays Moses: "The man Moses was very humble, above all the men who are on the face of the earth." This is the quality, above all others, to which the Torah called direct attention.

Nor is this an isolated tribute to the role of humility. It serves as the climax of Micah's eloquent summation of man's highest duties: "What doth the Lord require of thee? Only to do justice, to love mercy and to walk humbly with thy God."

In rabbinic writings also there are many impressive indications of how highly humility was cherished by the molders of our tradition. "Why was man created last in the order of Creation?" the sages ask. And they answer, "In order that, should he ever become too proud, he might be reminded that the tiniest flea preceded him in the divine scheme of things." In another *Midrash* we are told that God revealed himself to Moses in a lowly bush and not in a tall, stately tree, precisely because of the modest size of the bush. Again, he chose Sinai, the smallest of the mountains in that region, to teach us that humility is a requisite for experiencing God's presence. Elsewhere, we are told that the prophet Isaiah compared the words of the Torah to water, because, "just as water forsakes the high places and flows down to the low ones, so do the words of the Torah find a resting place only in a man of humble spirit." Another sage, Rabbi Levitas of Jabneh, counseled, "Be exceedingly humble, for what is the hope of mortals but the grave."

Does this mean that Judaism considers it sinful for a human being to feel a sense of pride? Scarcely. Who will condemn the look of quiet pride that settles on the faces of parents as their sons chant their Bar Mitzvah blessings and Haftorah? Who will question the right of a mother to be proud as her lovely daughter and her nervous husband come down the aisle leading to the canopy? The father who raises a decent family, the mother who prepares a tasty meal, the shoemaker who makes a beaten pair of shoes look wearable again, the secretary whose letter is neat and evenly spaced, the Jew who contemplates his inheritance and finds it noble—all these have their moments of pride, and who will challenge their right to them?

Moreover, there is often virtue in pride. A man may be too proud to demean himself. He may have too high an opinion of himself to resort to dishonesty or betrayal or compromise with principle. "Pride," it has been rightly said, "makes some men ridiculous and prevents others from becoming so." There is the kind of pride that prompts a man not to turn his nose up but to keep his chin up and to carry his honor high. When a Jew of yesterday was tempted to perform an unseemly act, he would instinctively protest: "Es passt nit far a yid—this is conduct unbecoming a Jew." His pride prevented him from debasing himself. Even the Chasidim, who valued humility so highly, taught that

161

there are moments when pride becomes a duty. "When the Evil Inclination approaches, whispering in your ear: 'You are unworthy to fulfill the Torah,' You must say: 'I am worthy.'" We all need a strong measure of such pride.

What our tradition opposes so strongly is the pride which causes a man to be so dazzled by the splendor of his own brilliance that he sees no one else; the pride which tempts a man into the blasphemy and folly of thinking of himself as a self-made man and worshipping his creator.

This, as our sages saw it, was the cardinal sin of Pharaoh, as indeed of all tyrants. He suffered from an inflated sense of his own importance. Pharaoh, our sages say, played the role of God. "Anee v'afsee od—There is none as exalted as I am."—he proclaimed. "The Nile is my own. I have made it for myself." It was, therefore, our sages say, that the first plague to be visited upon Egypt was the plague which turned the waters of the Nile into blood. This was designed to teach Pharaoh an object lesson in humility.

How shall we be saved from that kind of consuming pride? How can we derive satisfaction from our work without being blinded by a vision of ourselves? How can we cultivate a mood of humility in a society given to proclaiming aloud one's virtues— real and imaginary?

It seems to me that, in the first place, we have to maintain a sense of proportion and a sense of perspective.

Quite recently, after repeated failures, man finally conquered the forbidding heights of Mt. Everest. For a few brief moments of exaltation man stood on the top and looked down. It was, of course, a magnificent victory of the indomitable human spirit, which has refused to accept limits on its vast capacities.

And yet I wonder if ever a man had a right to feel any more insignificant than did those intrepid climbers alone in the howling vastness of space. Who among us has not stood on a mountain and felt, with the psalmist, an exaggerated awareness of our microscopic size? "When I behold the heavens, the work of Thy hands, the moon and the stars which Thou has created, what is man that Thou art mindful of him, or the son of man that Thou takest account of him?" How small they must have felt up there in their moment of greatest triumph. This is what Pascal had in mind when he said, "When he consults himself, man knows he is great. When he contemplates the universe around him, he knows that he is little and his ultimate greatness consists of his knowledge of his littleness." When we feel a powerful sense of our own importance creeping up on us, it might be very salutary to run for the nearest mountain.

Well, I suppose we might be ready to concede, in our more generous moments, that we are not as big as the infinite universe, but our pride usually feeds on the knowledge or the illusion that we are so much better than other people. The truth is that, in spite of the preamble to the Declaration of Independence, all men are not created equal. In George Orwell's "Nineteen Eighty-four," the worker's building displays an inscription which declares: "All men are equal only some men are more equal than others." There is a vast difference between a Heifetz and the usher who shows a ticket bearer to his seat in the concert hall. There is an enormous gap between a George Bernard Shaw and the salesgirl who sells his book in the department store. There is an impressive discrepancy between an Arthur Szyk who captured in color the grandeur and pathos of Jewish life and the man who buys the master's painting for his study. Seen through human eyes, we are indeed not equal at all.

And yet, before God, how small we all are! This, I believe, is why the prophet Micah suggested that we walk humbly with our God. When you walk with God it must be humbly. For what, after all, is the music of a Heifetz before Him Who taught the brooks to murmur, the leaves to whisper, the wind to howl, the birds to sing and the baby to cry? How impressive is a Shaw compared to the Divine Playwright whose dramas touch everything and whose cast of characters include every human being? How significant is the brush of a Szyk alongside the One who paints sunsets daily and touches the leaves of autumn with intoxicating colors? How large is our knowledge compared with

163

the Infinite wisdom? How big is our goodness alongside of the unspeakable mercy of God? "A mountain shames a molehill until they are both humbled by the stars." Phillips Brooks was dispensing very sound spiritual advice when he said, "The true way to be humble is not to stoop until you are smaller than yourself, but to stand at your real height against some higher nature that will show you what the real smallness of your greatness is."

This leaves one last point, which is perhaps most decisive. To every one of our accomplishments an infinite number of people, past and present, have made their contribution. Let us take an example that I know best—this sermon. Of course I wrote it myself. Well—almost myself.

In retrospect, I see that I have quoted the Bible, the Mishnah, the Talmud, a television star, Gilbert and Sullivan, Pascal and Brooks, among others. Apart from these, the sermon is all my own, except, of course, that there were certain Rebbes who taught me to read the Bible and the Talmud, and there were the teachers who taught me to read English. There were also some people who inspired me to become a rabbi. And then there is the small matter of some 150 generations of Jews who struggled to keep the tradition alive.

Oh, yes, it is difficult to preach at 9:45 p.m. on an empty stomach, so we ought to consider the Shabbat meal we ate before these late services tonight. There was the farmer who raised the chicken, the *Shochet* who slaughtered it, the butcher who sold it, the delivery boy who brought it, the *rebbetzin* who koshered it and cooked it, and our three daughters who made it tastier by their constant chatter. Shall I take you through the whole meal —wine, *challah*, vegetables, dessert and all? No less than eighty people are involved between the time that wheat is planted and a loaf of bread appears on my table.

In fairness, I suppose we ought to include also those who built the Synagogue and pulpit, those who provided the flowers, the heat, you trusting people who came to listen, the babysitters who released some of you. Shall I go on? Come to think of it, I have not even mentioned the most important ingredient that went into the preaching of this sermon, the health and strength I need to speak.

On second thought, many a hand wrote this sermon tonight, and if I cannot even write a sermon alone, how can I even in my most self-intoxicated moments dare to consider myself a self-made man?

Humility, then, is simply a matter of fairness, of getting our sights adjusted. We must learn to see ourselves in true relationship to the world, to our fellowman, and to God. If we get our spiritual lenses refracted we can then more easily follow the counsel of Jeremiah:

"Thus saith the Lord:

> Let not the wise man glory in his wisdom.
> Neither let the mighty man glory in his might.
> Neither let the rich man glory in his riches.
> But let him that glorieth glory in this:
> That he understandeth and knoweth me,
> That I am the Lord Who exercises mercy,
> Justice and righteousness in the earth
> For in these things I delight
> Saith the Lord."

Humbly let us pray:
Father of the strong and the weak before whom even the strongest is weak;
Lord of all wisdom and knowledge before whom even the wisest is as a speechless child;
Thou who dost fill the heavens and revealest thyself in a lowly bush;
Thou who dwellest in the high places and with him who is of a humble spirit;
Fill us with the pride that keeps us from self-humiliation,
Purge us from the pride which leads to self-exaltation.
Keep us mindful that we are only human,
So that we might be most human.

Impress upon us our littleness so that we may strive for true greatness.

Encourage us to measure ourselves against the stars so that we might be tempted to reach for them.

Help us to see how we lean upon Thee and upon one another so that we truly fulfill the injunction of Thy Prophet: "to do justice, love mercy and to walk humbly before Thee."

Amen.

FRANKLIN DELANO ROOSEVELT
A CHAPLAIN'S TRIBUTE

An appraisal of our fallen Commander-in-Chief delivered before a military congregation at Sabbath Eve services, on the day following his sudden death.

19

Franklin Delano Roosevelt -
A Chaplain's Tribute

"Hushed be the camps today
And soldiers, let us drape our war-worn weapons;
And each with musing soul retire to celebrate
Our dear commander's death.

No more for him life's stormy conflicts
Nor victory, nor defeat—no more time's dark events,
Charging like ceaseless clouds across the sky.

But sing poet in our name;
Sing of the love we bore him—because you, dweller in
Camps, know it truly.
As they invault the coffin there;
Sing—as they close the doors of the earth upon him—one verse
For the heavy hearts of soldiers."

Walt Whitman
(Upon the death of Abraham Lincoln)

SCARCELY twenty four hours have passed since a thick mourning shroud enveloped our entire nation. We are still too stunned by the suddenness of our overwhelming loss to be able to cast our gloom into words which will adequately express the deep personal sense of bereavement in which we all share. With poignant relevance does the rabbinical observation apply to the passing of Franklin Delano Roosevelt: "Chacham she-met hakol krovav—

when a wise man dies all are his relations." Our mourning today is not only intimately personal, it is also universal. We have each lost a close friend; our Armed Forces have lost their Commander-in-Chief; our nation has lost its President; humanity has lost its champion.

The tragedy of our President's death is deepened by its untimeliness. How sorely the United Nations shall miss his vision and his leadership during the coming months! How richly he deserved to taste the fruits of victory over Nazism—fruits of which he was the chief planter and which are now virtually ripe for the plucking. In millions of aching hearts there is a gnawing rhetorical question: "Why couldn't he have lived just a little longer?" It is almost inevitable that the painful biblical analogy of the untimely death of Moses should insinuate itself into our thoughts at this moment. Moses, too, had transcended a physical handicap to assume leadership of his people. He too led them through critical, perilous years, inspiring them with courage and his leadership, battling their doubts, buttressing their faith and keeping steadfastly before them the vision of the ultimate, single objective— the Promised Land. When finally the Promised Land appears within view, when the threshold of realization is reached, Moses is permitted only a glimpse of the Promised Land from the distance before death rudely intervenes to claim him.

I recall the sense of rebellion that filled me when, as a child, I read this biblical story for the first time. How cruel was the sense of frustration I felt for Moses. To have struggled so long for an overarching goal only to be denied its attainment at the precise moment when it was virtually within reach. Ah! that was too disheartening a climax to the story of a great human adventure. It seemed to betray the very faith which Moses himself had lived. It seemed to empty the vision which Moses had so resolutely championed.

With maturity, however, the sense of rebellion was mellowed by the realization that in the apparently premature death of Moses the Bible was conveying an inescapable truth of human experience. The great always die too soon. For it is in the essence

170

of greatness that it sets up for itself goals which are too all-embracing to be achieved in any lifetime however long, its objectives are too far-reaching to be realized in any single life-span. Every Moses inevitably leaves his final Jordan uncrossed and must rest content with only a glimpse of his Promised Land.

Franklin Delano Roosevelt could never have accomplished all his humanitarian tasks. As long as man hungered for bread anywhere, as long as man wore the shackles of servitude anywhere, as long as man suffered persecution or walked in the shadow of fear anywhere, his work would have remained undone. Whenever death would have claimed him, it would have found him in the midst of some unfinished human symphony. Let this thought temper our sadness tonight.

We may find additional comfort, and at the same time better appreciate the great spirit that moved among us, if we dwell not upon the circumstances of his death, but rather upon the quality of his life. We are still too close to the scene of his momentous accomplishments to be able to evaluate properly their full import upon human history. A future historian equipped with the perspective that time alone affords, will record the full measure of President Roosevelt's legacy to man's spiritual endowment. But ours has been the unique privilege of being his contemporaries. As such we have had the opportunity to be his co-workers for a more abundant world. Under his inspiration, we fought against greed and selfishness at home so that the manifold blessings with which nature has so lavishly endowed America might be enjoyed by the many rather than the few. Under the banner of his leadership, we overcame our differences and welded this nation into a mighty fighting force which is now battling on a hundred battlefields so that freedom and human dignity might be the common lot of all men. Through the magic of his eloquence we were aroused to the realization that democracy, to survive, had to cease being a way of speaking and become a dynamic, purposeful way of living. Tonight let us be thankful that we were the America that President Roosevelt led. Let us mingle the grief over his death with gratitude for his noble life.

We find solace also in the dictum of our Sages who said: *"Tsadikim b'mitatam k'ruim chayim*—the righteous even in death are called living."* In a deep and noble sense, the great never cease to endure as a living influence among humanity. Moses does enter into the Promised Land with his people. Though physically removed from them, he enters with them in their hearts, in their hopes, in their strivings. He has become indelibly impressed upon their national and individual consciousness, woven into the very web of their existence.

President Roosevelt will live in the victory which we shall score over tyranny and barbarism. His spirit will be with us in San Francisco and at all conferences where men of good will gather to plot the lasting peace he worked for and wherever men assemble to build the world of simple justice, kindness and righteousness which he envisioned. His guiding genius will be as real to us in the Promised Land as his dynamic personality was in the wilderness through which he led us.

It is our human custom to insure against the failings of human memory by erecting monuments to perpetuate the great who stir among us for a few fleeting moments before they are claimed by the ages. Undoubtedly, we shall rear impressive marble figures to President Roosevelt. But the greatest and most enduring monument to his memory, he himself has already built not alone in the hearts of his countrymen but in the hearts of all men everywhere who aspire to life's blessings. He more than any other person symbolized the truths for which we fight. He more than any other person articulated the dreams of the underprivileged, the weak, humanity's common men who found in him their indefatigable champion. These shall ever gratefully kindle the flame of his memory in the fireplace of posterity.

If we would truly pay tribute to our fallen leader, let us do so not by words alone but by deeds as well. Let us first strive with a common and resolute will to hasten the end of the war which he waged with exemplary courage and determination. And when the furies of war are spent and peace is restored to a sadder but wiser humanity, may we prove capable of patterning America after those ideals which he held sacred. Let us make of it a better and more beautiful America which will lead in the search of a happier world—a world that will not have to pay for its mistakes with the lives of its youth, a world where all men shall be equal and all men shall be free, a world in which each man will sit under his own vine and his own fig tree and there shall be none to make him afraid. For only as these things come to pass shall President Roosevelt's visions be clothed with flesh, his dreams become living substance. In that better world his spirit will live and never perish from the hearts of men.

As we commit his sacred soul to the hands of God who loaned it to mankind, we pray in the words our President used in his message to the Armed Forces at the end of 1943: "We ask that God receive and cherish him who has given his life, and that we keep him in honor and in the grateful memory of his countrymen, forever."   Amen.

THE MEANING OF ISRAEL

A salute to Israel on the first Rosh Hashanah in the life of
the infant state and an attempt to indicate its impact on the
life of the American Jew.

Preached on Rosh Hashanah, 1948

20

The Meaning of Israel

TODAY we usher in the year 5709 on the Jewish calendar and the year one in the life of the third Jewish Commonwealth— the State of Israel. Because this is the first Rosh Hashanah in the life of reborn Israel we cannot permit it to pass without pausing to evaluate its meaning and its impact upon world Jewry.

I limit myself to world Jewry although I have full confidence that Israel will leave a deep and lasting imprint on all of subsequent human history—not upon Jewish history alone. If the history of our people indicates anything at all, it demonstrates that greatness has nothing to do with bigness. If we took a large map of the Western world including America, Europe and the Western part of Asia, the city of Jerusalem would be represented in the lower right hand corner on that map by an almost invisible speck. Yet the entire religious culture and the spiritual legacy of the rest of that map was born and nurtured in that tiny spot. I have strong faith that what will happen in that little land from now on will have a tremendous influence on the rest of the world. But it will take a future chronicler to evaluate that influence and to record it. For the present, let us merely try to understand the meaning of infant Israel to our people in the far-flung corners of the globe.

Every Jewish boy of Bar Mitzvah age has already lived through in his short life-time two monumental episodes in Jewish history. The first was an unprecedented cataclysm of destruction and decimation; the second was the unparalleled miracle of rebuilding and rebirth. Who knows—perhaps there is no connection between these two events. Perhaps it is just a coincidence that the death

175

throes of the six million should have been so closely followed by the birth pangs of Israel. Or perhaps there was more truth than we suspected in the legend our fathers told that the Messiah would come only when the cup of Jewish tears was filled to overflowing. In any event, ours has been the generation singled out by destiny to witness first with unspeakable horror and then with unexpressable joy, death and birth in the household of Israel. In a long, long history charged with drama and pathos it is most remarkable that two of its most decisive events, such completely contrasting events, should be telescoped into what is barely a moment on the clock of Jewish history. Ours is the generation of whom Chaim Nachman Bialik spoke: "*Dor acharon l'shibud; dor rishon lig'ulah*—the last generation of bondage; the first generation of redemption."

Both of the historic events of our time have cut very deeply into the consciousness of world Jewry. No Jew anywhere can today pretend that these events have not registered a profound impression, consciously or otherwise, upon his attitude towards himself, towards his people and towards the world in which he lives. Both these events have tended to eliminate the Jew who as late as the early thirties tried to delude himself with the belief that his Jewishness was no more significant either to himself or to society than the color of his hair. Both these events have made of the Jewish identity an enormous fact to be reckoned with. In the mass anonymous Jewish graves that dot the continent of Europe, there were also laid to rest the ghosts of the indifferent Jews. Among the vast audience now warmly applauding the heroic exploits of the *Yishuv* we must also include the Jew who didn't know he cared.

In spite of the apparent similarities between these two epoch-making events in their psychological impact upon the mind of the Jew, there is actually a world of difference between them. And it is in the difference that the real significance of Israel lies. In the difference we must seek the clue to the meaning of Israel to you and to me.

The first very vital difference between the effect of the death

176

of the six million and the amazing triumph of Israel is this: While the first emphasized the *penalty* of being Jewish, the second emphasized the *pride* of being Jewish. Nazism served to frighten Jews back to the fold with such doleful slogans as, "It can happen here, you know," . . . "If we don't hang together, we'll hang separately." Such catchwords, whatever their truth, did serve to double and treble membership in Bnai Brith lodges, in Jewish protective agencies, in Zionist groups and even in synagogue organizations. They helped Jewish fund-raising efforts beyond estimate. But they hardly could have been expected to bolster Jewish morale. Indeed, if the plethora of books by Jewish authors dealing with anti-Semitism is any indication, it would seem that Nazism served to awaken not so much Jewish consciousness as Jewish self-conciousness. It underscored the liability of being Jewish and who can tell whether those whom it frightened back to the fold were not outnumbered by those whom it frightened out of the fold.

Far different has been the exhilarating mood imbued by the rebirth of Israel and the astonishing victories that made it possible. Israel has taken the "*krechtz*" out of Jewish living! It has given Jews everywhere a mighty banner around which to rally— a banner not a tombstone. It has made Jews everywhere feel, as did our fathers for other reasons, that being a Jew is a proud privilege.

A few examples come boldly to mind. One is the simple statement of one of our young girls, a student at Junior High School. Shortly after May 15th I asked her whether there was any discussion of Israel in her classes. "Yes," she said "everybody was talking about it in our current events class." She paused for a moment, then added, "You know, rabbi, it's a funny thing, before I used to feel very uncomfortable when any teacher spoke about Jews. But now, I'm very proud about it. And what's more a lot of the kids in school now say 'we' when they refer to Jews." This comment speaks volumes for the new sense of dignity Israel is giving to every Jew old enough to think and feel.

Another illustration. In a lead editorial entitled, "Morale,"

177

the American Hebrew pointed out a few weeks ago that Israel has profoundly changed the key in which the poetry of its contributors is being written. In the past, it says, "the usual run of verse dripped tears in endless rivulets over the ancient hard lot of the Jewish people. . . . But there has been a remarkable and gratifying change now in the tone of the verse received. It is full of courage, of joy, of fortitude, of energy . . . and the stream of tears has about dried up."

A specific example is Karl Shapiro, by fairly common consent the most gifted of the younger American poets. Until a few months ago he was cited prominently as illustrating a tendency to total assimilation in American Jewry. In fact, his recent poetry echoed Christian motifs and reflected Jewish self-hatred. Again and again he struck out against his people. But came the birth of Israel and within a month Karl Shapiro wrote in the New Yorker: "When I think of the liberation of Zion, I hear the drop of chains . . . I feel the weight of prisons in my skull falling away. . . . When I see the name of Israel high in print the fences crumble in my flesh . . . I say my name aloud for the first time unconsciously. . . . Speak the name of the land, speak the name only of the living land."

Yes, "the name of the living land," and this alone, could awaken the dormant yearning in estranged Jewish hearts. Worldly Jews, lukewarm Jews arise today as never before and with one voice and one will re-ally themselves with their people. Jews everywhere have heard the drop of chains and have felt the weight of prisons fall away. They walk the earth with a newly discovered sense of pride and self-respect. In brief, Israel will not only take many Jews out of exile; it has already taken the exile out of the Jew. That is the first meaning of Israel.

Israel has done something more for us—something so subtle that it could easily be overlooked. It has reversed the 2000 year old role of the Jew on the stage of history. For the past two millenia the Jew's external history has been shaped for him by other nations. He moved when he was told to go, he remained when he was prevented from going. How far he could walk from his home was determined by the size of the ghetto area, the occupations in which he could engage, were decided by the ruling powers. Coercion, subjugation, oppression, persecution, exile, martyrdom—these were the involuntary roles assigned to him. The script-writers changed but the part assigned to the Jew was always the same. Jewish history—except of course in the spiritual realm—has been for 2,000 years not the story of what the Jew did as much as what was done to him. This motif of helplessness and passivity reached its frightening crescendo in the death of the six million. Behold the Jew! The great and glorious *"nebechel"* on the world's stage.

Seen against this back-ground, the rebirth of Israel and the fifty years of stubborn pioneering that preceded it and made it possible, point to a new role that the Jew has chosen for himself. He is saying to the world: "No more shall my destiny be shaped by the unkind hands of others. No longer shall I dance to the mocking tunes played by alien instruments. I have had enough— dear world too much—of playing the anvil for your hammer blows. Once upon a time my ancestors called themselves Maccabees because *"Maccab"* means a hammer. Once again I shall beat out my own destiny, I shall forge for myself the instruments of my salvation. With men of good will the world over I shall cooperate in the building of a better society. But I shall cooperate as an equal not as a beggar waiting at the banquet tables of the mighty for a crumb of kindness. And until the blessed day of understanding among peoples arrives, I shall honestly, stubbornly and unflinchingly rebuild myself in body and spirit on my ancestral soil which bloomed when my fathers tilled it, lay waste for centuries in alien hands and which has awakened once more to the tender caress of loving hands."

That is the meaning of Israel. That is the central meaning. A people is on the march, not a forced march, but a self-willed march. It has gotten off its knees and straightened its shoulders stooped by the burdens of the long night of exile and is standing erect. The spirit of the Maccabees has been rekindled. Israel has redeemed not only the land but more especially itself.

Finally the rebirth of Israel has meant the rebirth of our faith in the power of ideals. It has reaffirmed our faith in the reality of spiritual forces in the world. It has rekindled our belief in miracles.

Who would have dared to believe possible only fifty years ago what we have seen with our own eyes? Yes, an impractical, starry-eyed dreamer by the name of Herzl said it would come to pass but any "realistic" student of history could have advanced a thousand cogent reasons to deny the possibility of such a consummation. For here was a people divorced from its land for almost 2000 years, exposed to the corrosive acids of human brutality, a people whose very existence was called into question by historians who labelled it a "fossil," a people whose dreams of restoration had been mocked by circumstance and even repudiated by many of its own members. That such a people could achieve the fulfillment of its most cherished and long-deferred hope at the precise moment when the hand of despair lay most heavily upon it—this is an achievement to convert the most skeptical and cynical of men into passionate believers in the invincibility of the human spirit when wedded to an imperishable ideal.

A philosopher who was once challenged to point to a miracle is said to have answered simply: "The Jews." It was their survival to which he was referring. How else shall we designate our people's collective revival except as a miracle?

An old prophecy has been fulfilled with almost uncanny literalness. We recall that powerfully moving 37th chapter of the book of Ezekiel. Ezekiel who prophecied during the Babylonian exile tells of being taken into a valley strewn with human skeletons. As he beholds the forbidding and hopeless sight, the voice of God asks him: "Can these dry bones come to life?" Ezekiel doesn't dare answer "yes." So God tells him: "Therefore prophesy and say to the people. Thus saith the Lord God: 'Behold I shall open your graves' and I shall raise you up out of your graves, my people, and I shall bring you upon the land of Israel."

Can we think of a more appropriate description of what has

happened in our own days? A people rising out of Europe's graveyards, dry bones coming to life!

And an ancient rabbi provided some remarkable details for this prophecy. Rabbi Elazar taught: "The Holy One blessed be He will make subterannean tunnels for them and they will roll until they reach the Land of Israel. When they reach the land of Israel the Lord will infuse them with the spirit of life and they shall stand erect!"

Here you have an adumbration of the whole underground passage to Israel that took place during the last few years.

In the face of a miracle of such incredible dimensions our will to believe receives most powerful stimulation. If dried out bones can come to life before our eyes, are there indeed any miracles too wonderful for God to perform? With the rebirth of Israel there has been reborn the faith of decent men and women everywhere that God is not mocked, that ultimately it is "not by might and not by power but by My spirit saith the Lord of Hosts."

Thus, on this the first Rosh Hashanah in the life of Israel we salute our brethren. We say to them: "Thank you for making us proud of you and thereby restoring to us our sense of pride. Thank you too for charting a new and more dignified role for our people—the role of a people determined to forge its own glorious destiny in justice and equity. And above all thank you for reviving our faith in all that is beautiful and worthwhile in life."

To our gratitude we add the prayer that we may share with you in the noble task of the redemption of Israel, for by so doing—by standing erect and with dignity by your side, by matching your sacrifice with our strength we shall also redeem ourselves.

THE PEOPLE OF ISRAEL LIVES

A first-hand report on the State of Israel after a prolonged visit.
Its pressing problems and perils, its impressive advances and
achievements are spelled out in human terms.

Preached on Rosh Hashanah, 1955

21

The People of Israel Lives

OUR sages tell us that the Almighty gave the children of Israel three excellent gifts but they were each accompanied by a great deal of pain and anguish. One of these gifts was the Land of Israel which I was privileged to touch and tread upon for some four months. During my absence many of you marked joyous occasions, some of you sustained family losses. I don't mind confessing to you that your *simchas* made me homesick, your sorrows made me heartsick. All of you were kind enough to forego my services so that my family and I might realize the fulfillment of a yearning which was even denied Moses, who could see the land only from afar. By way of discharging in some measure the gratefulness which we feel to our congregation, I should like, on this day of Rosh Hashanah, to leave with you some of the impressions the Holy Land left with me.

To put it in capsule form, I would say: "I came, I saw, I was conquered." And let me tell you why.

May I begin with the story of Devorah Goldenberg, who for me personifies the spirit of re-born Israel. Soon after our arrival in Jerusalem we went to visit the Hadassah Hospital. On one of the walls we saw a series of ten vividly painted scenes depicting the life of the children in the hospital from the time they arise until they retire. The last scene was signed by the artist, Devorah Goldenberg—age 8. Our guide told us Devorah's story.

During the war of liberation touched off by the Arab's refusal to accept the United Nations' partition plan, a bomb exploded in Devorah's home in Jerusalem, instantly killing both her parents and blowing off Devorah's right arm. Jerusalem at the time was under constant heavy artillery bombardment to which the Jews could answer only by rifles—a most one-sided dialogue of death. The city was almost completely cut off from the rest of the country, without water, food, electricity and drugs. People were dying from superficial leg wounds for lack of these elementary necessities. But somehow, Devorah's life was saved in the hospital by surgeons equal to the task. The paintings we saw were done by Devorah after she learned how to use her left arm. Today. Devorah is the recipient of a Hadassah Scholarship and is a student at the Bezalel Institute of Art.

Devorah is symbolic of Israel—its severe handicaps and oppressive burdens, its indomitable courage, its faith in the future. If Israel is indeed a gift from the Almighty, it is certainly one with some very heavy strings attached. Let us consider first the elementary problem of sheer physical survival.

Israel looms very large in our consciousness but on the map it is actually a microscopic spot. For all its enormous history it has astoundingly little geography. Would you be surprised to learn that the entire State of Israel occupies an area of about 8,000 square miles, or less than the state of Massachusetts, or 1/70th of 1% of the total land surface of the globe? Of this meager land, more than half is the arid, desert land of the Negev and two hundred square miles consists of inland waters. This is the land which the Arabs consider too large for Israel. The seven Arab States which invaded Israel in 1948 comprise 1,200,000 square miles of territory or 150 times as much as Israel. If we include the entire Arab world, we have an area of four and a half million square miles—one and a half times the size of the United States.

Now, for all its lack of size, Israel's peculiar shape gives it 750 miles of frontier by land and sea. On all sides except the Mediterranean Sea, which has managed to stay neutral, Israel is bounded by enemies still smarting under their ignominious defeat of 1948 and openly vowing to destroy her. As recently as June 7th, the official radio mouthpiece of the Government of Egypt announced: "We cannot always remain in a state of war with Israel. We are, therefore, compelled to mobilize all Arab potential to exterminate her finally. Therefore, let us plant in the heart of the younger generation a hatred of Israel."

In the face of such threats to her existence, Israel, who enjoys no mutual defense pact with any other nation, has no choice but to support a large standing army, navy and air force, and to keep her veterans in a constant state of mobilization. Can we fully appreciate what a drain this preparedness imposes upon a country whose population numbers less than two million souls?

And who are the people of Israel? In 1948, when the State was proclaimed, there were 660,000 Jews. In the seven years which have elapsed, the Yishuv admitted 755,000 immigrants. The magnitude of this number can be better appreciated if we translate the proportions into the framework of the American population. If America were to accept a proportionate number of immigrants in the next seven years, it would mean adding a staggering 180 million to our present population of 160 million. And Israel, of course, is devoid of the extravagant resources with which America has been blessed.

From where did the immigrants come? To answer a question in Jewish style, by asking a question—From where did they not come? One has only to take a short ride in an Israeli bus to realize the full scope of the ingathering. The various shades of skin, including the jet black of the Abyssinian Jew, the different modes of dress reflecting both European and Oriental origins, the variety of dialects among the newcomers—all equally unintelligible to my American-Hebrew ears—these serve to dramatize the fact that Israel has more than fulfilled Isaiah's prophecy: "From the East will I bring they seed and from the West will I gather thee." Indeed, as you look upon and listen to the motley aggregate on the bus, you have to pull yourself up short and remind yourself that they are all Jews—your brothers. The Kurdistani may still be wearing his balloon-like trousers, the Indian Jewess may not yet have discarded her long flowing robes, or the daughter of Iran her heavily beaded headdress. For all the differences in attire, in language, in background, they have come to Israel in search of something they could find nowhere else.

Now, these immigrants come not only from different places, they also from different centuries. The Jew who comes from Germany comes from the 20th century. The Jew who comes from Yemen comes from the Middle Ages. His wife, when she is having a baby, which is almost always, has to be lured into a hospital, taught how to light a stove, dress a baby and feed it, and must be introduced to that mysterious utensil we call a "fork." She has come from a country which is accustomed to burying its infants. I remember vividly a Yemenite Jew who told me that he had two surviving grown children out of eighteen who were born to his wife. His grandchildren will be born in a country which has the lowest infant mortality rate in that part of the world.

Among the writings left by F. Scott Fitzgerald there was found the theme for a story which he meant to write one day. It was to be about a widely separated family which has inherited a large house in which they must now live together. Fitzgerald never wrote that story, but in Israel that story is in fact now being acted out.

Somehow all these people have to learn to live together. In one tiny country, a bridge must be built across the centuries, diverse social and cultural backgrounds must be merged and, if differences cannot be obliterated quickly, at least they have to be accepted and tolerated. We in America have proudly referred to our country as a "melting pot" for the various peoples who came here. Israel is too harassed to afford the luxury of waiting for the different strains to blend in a "melting pot." Israel has to be a pressure cooker.

What did these people bring with them besides their hopes and dreams? Of worldly possessions almost nothing. But among Israel's unwanted imports we must list many diseases they brought with them. Trachoma, tuberculosis, ringworm, hookworm and many other such afflictions which are common in the underprivileged two-thirds of humanity. Israel is addressing itself to these health problems with its characteristic vigor and determination. In one of the immigrant camps, for example, trachoma was reduced in four months from an incidence of 98% to 20%.

But these are not the only afflictions which need healing. There are others which were brought by the remnants of Hitler's crematoria, gas-chambers and concentration camps. These survivors can be identified outwardly by the numbers the Nazis tattooed on their arms. They don't wash off. But what hurts and memories do they carry within, and what serum do you use for such afflictions? The healing they need is subtle and slow. Taken together, all these people must be rebuilt, rehabilitated and made productive.

If we understand the melancholy burdens these immigrants have brought with them, we can better understand why Israel is so anxious to have a large *Aliyah* of American Jews. We are not afflicted by disease, nor scarred by bitter memories, nor handicapped by ignorance and poverty. Israel is most anxious that we come in sizeable numbers. The first question you are asked in Israel when they see you are American, and somehow there is no hiding it, even if you speak Hebrew and wear shorts, is: "Are you planning to remain? Did you come to settle?" Israel needs our money, is gratified by our moral and political support, is pleased by our kind words. But they would say to us: "Immigration is the sincerest form of flattery." How to stimulate American immigration is now being given some very earnest consideration.

These, then, are some of the problems which baby Israel faces. How to keep alive amidst hostile neighbors threatening to commit infanticide, how to give healing and sustenance to the newly gathered members of her family, how indeed to weld them into a family group.

For all these problems, my dominant impression of Israel is this: Though it is bent under the weight of many burdens it can straighten the back of any Jew. Nowhere else in the world could I get a stronger feeling of the pulsating, living reality which we call the Jewish people than I got in Israel. There you know that our people is throbbing and vital and dynamic. When you are there, the words "Am Yisrael chai—the People of Israel lives," are not a pious wish or a rhetorical flourish. It is a simple, inescapable description of fact.

Professor Toynbee in an eight-volume study dedicated to the birth and dissolution of civilizations, has little room for or patience with the Jewish people. "The Jews," he writes, "are fossils of the Syriac society." A fossil in science, is a petrified remnant like the shell which lingers on even though the spirit which once infused it with life has fled. Professor Toynbee only demonstrates that scholarship is often no antidote to prejudice. For if the Jewish people are a fossil then I dare say they have remained singularly unaware of their own demise and constitute the most active, living fossils on record. If the professor could lift his head from his scholarly tomes for an instant and examine this fossil, he would find in it a most remarkable resiliency and vitality.

Let us list some of the more conspicuous evidences of the pulsating life that courses through the veins of Israel. For one thing, Israel speaks.

I believe that it was Eliezer ben Yehuda, whose story has been so sympathetically retold in Robert St. John's "Tongue of The Prophets," who said, "a people that lives speaks; a people that speaks lives."

We were made aware of the rebirth of the language as soon as we settled down in our El Al plane in London. Before take off, a sign lit up telling us to tighten our safety belts and refrain from smoking—in Hebrew. Our hostess was Yardena—whose very name announces that the land is yielding not only nourishment but also Hebrew nomenclature. The sugar wrapper, the cellophane utensil package, the instructions over the intercom—all breathe Hebrew. Having arrived in Israel, of course, you enter into a Hebraic universe of discourse. Some new immigrants have not yet discarded their native tongues but already their children are speaking Hebrew and will teach it to them. Mothers are learning the mother tongue from their children, and every day necessities will hasten the process.

I remember one day standing at a teller's window in a bank in Haifa and overhearing the man in front of me repeatedly asking, in German, for change of a check. The teller kept asking him

188

in Hebrew what he was saying, and the man kept repeating his request in German. Becoming somewhat impatient, I translated his request to the teller into Hebrew. But the teller shot back at me, "I know German too, but I know that he knows Hebrew and I want him to use it."

Nor is it only Jews who are speaking Hebrew in Israel. I remember a conversation with a French prirest who was in charge of the Theological School, the Ratisbonne, in Jerusalem. The language which issued from the throat surrounded by a turned white starch collar was Hebrew. He had to know Hebrew to be able to perform his duties in Israel.

After long centuries of being compelled to learn the tongues of the nations among whom we dwelled, there is something secretly gratifying to find other nations being compelled to learn our language—the language in which Israel is creating new dramas, singing new songs, writing a new literature, and saying such trite things as: "*Mah shlomchah?*"—how are you?" or, "*mah hasha'ah?*—what time is it?" The tongue of the prophets has become the language of the plumber and policeman too. The sacred tongue in which the Jew used to speak only to God he now uses also in speaking to his brothers. Eliezer ben Yehuda's prophecy has been vindicated: "Among the miracles of Jewish history the revival of the Hebrew language in our day will stand out for generations as the greatest and most wonderful." When you hear the remarkable revival of Hebrew, you know that "*Am Yisrael chai*, the People of Israel lives."

And your back becomes a little straighter if you watch, as we did, the military parade on *Yom Atzma'ut*—Israel's July 4th on the 5th of Iyar. In my military experience I had witnessed enough parades to last me a lifetime, I thought. But somehow we were walking on air when we left the Ramat Gan stadium after watching the review that day. Fifty thousand people had jammed the stadium and when the loud-speaker announced to the blare of trumpets "The President of the State of Israel," the crowd cheered wildly with the pent-up pride of the centuries.

On the field were hundreds of bearded paratroopers under

their red berets, a contingent of sharp looking and trimly dressed women soldiers, foot soldiers, Israeli sailors and air corps boys. And when the order sounded to present arms, they executed it with a precision that reflected the utmost discipline and training. Tanks rumbled by, planes flew overhead, marching maneuvers were held and your chest swelled when you said to yourself this is a Jewish parade of the first Jewish army in two millenia and these are the boys and girls whose heroism had given birth to the State and covered themselves with sparkling glory. In your heart you prayed that they might never have to use those weapons again, but you felt secure in the knowledge that, if there were to be a next time, Israel would not be found unprepared.

And who were the people watching? Apart from the tourists, almost every one who was in Israel in 1948 had made a personal sacrifice in the war. The fellow who drove us in the taxi had an artificial right arm to replace the one he lost in Ramat Rachel. The man in the row in front of us was missing two legs. A woman who sat behind us pointed proudly to her nephew who was throwing a snappy salute as he marched by the reviewing stand, and then she added quietly in Hebrew: "He's the only one left from his family."

Independence in Israel has been dearly purchased. It will not be surrendered.

There is another aspect of Israel which must be entered on the credit side of the ledger and which strikes you very forcefully —that is the occupational normalization of Jewish life.

Israel consists of people who, in the lands of the dispersion, showed an abnormal concentration in the professions, in white collar jobs and in merchandizing. That there are valid historical reasons for this occupational imbalance is well known. But the fact is that it was abnormal and in many instances extremely provocative. It served as grist in the mill of the anti-Semite who could clothe with seeming truth his lie that the Jew was a parasite and was incapable of productive labor.

Israel has hurled this taunt into the face of our detractors. There, ditches are dug—by Jews. Shoes are made, repaired and

190

shined—by Jews. The barren, stubborn, neglected soil is reclaimed, ploughed, planted, harvested—by Jews. Newspapers are written, printed, sold on street corners—by Jews. Electricity is being generated—by Jews, sent over wires strung—by Jews, on poles erected by Jews, into homes built by Jews, into sockets manufactured and installed by Jews, to be used in appliances made by Jews. The mechanic who services your car, the policeman who gives you a ticket for driving it too fast, the judge who sentences you, and the jailer who may have to keep an eye on you—they are all Jews.

In brief, every imaginable service is being rendered by Jews. There is a new dignity to labor. When Bartley Crum visited the Displaced Persons Camps, one of the men showed him his hands and said: "You see these hands. They haven't worked. . . . All we're praying for is the opportunity to build our own homes and to put these hands back to work again."

Well, the hands are working and when you see them behind a tractor or a plough or a shovel you understand the deep meaning of the song—"*Anu banu artza livnot u-l'hibanot bah*—we have come to the land to build and to be re-built in it." In the factories, on the farms, in the cities, you see that "*Am Yisrael chai*— the People of Israel lives."

And need I spell out in detail the most remarkable achievements our people have wrought in Israel? At the opening of the present century, Clarence Darrow wrote: "Palestine is a land of sand and stones and the stones are there to keep the sand from blowing away." Nobody could have foretold then that the land, long dead, choked beneath the hot desert sands that had been permitted to suffocate it, was destined for a marvelous resurrection. It seems indeed that "the land without a people was waiting for the people without a land." Stubbornly, patiently, courageously, lovingly, the Jew has reclaimed his beloved soil. He washed away her salt and sand. He drained her marshes and swamps. He wiped out her malaria and trachoma. He diverted rivers and tunneled mountains. He has healed the scars of century-old neglect.

By 1948, the *Yishuv* had built 277 agricultural settlements. In the seven years since the State was established, another 420

191

have been added. The growth in industry, homebuilding, road-building, has been equally spectacular. A tribute to Jewish achievement came recently from an unexpected source. An Arab columnist writing in a Jordanian newspaper complained: "The Jews have made no promise they have not implemented. They said they would drain the Huleh swamps—and the swamps are dry. They said they would carry water from the Jordan and the Yarkon to the Negev—and the water is now flowing to the Negev. The Arabs knows only how to protest. We proclaimed we would oppose these actions by force but in the end the Jews got what they wanted and the Arabs nothing."

A friend of mine in Jerusalem gave me one night a graphic picture of Jewish industry and creativeness. He took me out to the balcony of his home and, pointing in the direction of the Israeli-Trans-Jordan border, he said: "Look there. You see the electric lights. That's Jewish Jerusalem. Beyond that you see darkness. That's Arab territory."

That, in essence, summed up in one image the truth that *Am Yisrael chai*—the People of Israel lives.

For last, I have left what to many of us must appear as Israel's most impressive appeal to Jews everywhere. It was put to me very pointedly by a former Philadelphian who is now serving as an expert in Israel on chicken farming. "There is one thing," he said, "that Israel has more of than any other country in the world, and that is the freedom to be Jewish." For most of Israel's Jews the freedom and security that Israel offers are in sharp contrast to the vile persecution and open discrimination which they endured in the lands of their origin. Did you know that in Yemen a Jew could not build a house more than two stories high so that he might not be able to look down upon a Moslem? Or that every orphan became the property of the State and was forced to convert to Islam? For them, of course, physical freedom is a blessing they are enjoying for the first time. But even for the Jew from democratic countries, where political freedom and equality are guaranteed, Israel has its distinctive appeal.

I think of the handsome young chemical engineer from the

Bronx whom I asked the obvious question: "What brought you to Israel?" His answer was very simple. "Here I could be sure that my Jewishness wouldn't count against me when I looked for a job and here I could be sure that I wouldn't have to work on Shabbat."

There are some other things you can be sure of in Israel if you are concerned with living as a Jew. You can be sure that the environment is your ally. Your child in public school will not only speak Hebrew, he will study the Bible—our Bible—Mishnah, Talmud, the history and literature of our people, the geography of Israel. The holidays he will observe will be our holidays and when he absents himself from school on those days, the schools will be closed to all. He will feel none of the tensions of being a member of a minority group whose sensitivities are sometimes trampled upon by thoughtless members of the majority or at best are simply overlooked. He will wear his Jewishness naturally, as naturally, say, as the child of the white Protestant here wears his Christianity. He may be more religious or less religious, depending on his home and training. But Jewishness will not be something over which he must forever soliloquize like an undecided Hamlet! "To be or not to be. . . ." He will be a Jew as naturally as he is a human being. For to him, Am Yisrael chai is a simple description of the basic fact of his life.

In Israel today the Hebrew word "nes—miracle," has been taken to stand for "neshek sodee—secret weapon." Israel's secret weapons have been a whole series of miracles. In Israel they say, "If you don't believe in miracles, you're no realist." You ask them how they won the war and they shrug their shoulders and tell you—a miracle from heaven. You ask yourself how a battered and tattered remnant could move so quickly from unprecedented decimation to unequalled achievement, from the abyss of agony to new heights of accomplishment, and you must answer—"nes gadol hayah po—a great miracle happened here." Then you know that no ordinary yardsticks can be applied to Israel. You have to measure it in history and prayers, in biblical prophesies and haunting dreams. It is a country with a romance—the greatest love story ever told—the love of a people for a land, the love of a land for a people. It was reclaimed by a people who have known death and outwitted it and who have returned home in remembrance of the ancient promise, "Unto thy seed shall I give this land."

It was Menachem Ussishkin who said: "Israel is a tiny land. The Jews are a tiny people. When the tiny people will re-settle the tiny land, great things will happen." This was certainly true in the past when our people created in Israel spiritual monuments vastly disproportionate to its size. Who will dare to predict it will not happen again? But we need not venture into the realm of prophecy. The magnificent achievements to date suffice to make every Jew fiercely proud of the great things done in this tiny land by a tiny but dedicated people.

Am Yisrael chai—the People of Israel lives!

IRON CURTAINS

Iron Curtains have been used throughout history to exclude the Jew. His response was to become a builder of bridges. Some of these important bridges are in desperate need of repairs.

Preached on *Kol Nidre*, 1948

22

Iron Curtains

NO recent figure of speech has struck such deep roots in the contemporary American mind as Winston Churchill's picturesque phrase, "The Iron Curtain." But while the phrase may be new, the phenomenon which it describes is as old as man himself. It is a melancholy truth that of all the blunderings of the human species few have been so frequent and so costly as the destructive tendency to build Iron Curtains—Iron Curtains of hatred and prejudice, dividing men of different religions, races, economic classes and social groups, and even natives from immigrants.

The Jew in particular can appreciate the full tragedy of Iron Curtains because on whatever boundaries they were lowered he almost invariably found himself on the wrong side. If religion was the issue, he became the victim of crusades and inquisitions. If, as in modern times, the racial question was raised, some sociologists could be persuaded to teach that he belonged to an inferior race and that he be made to suffer the consequences of that untruth. If the curtain was erected on economic boundaries, the Jew found his choice of an occupation severely limited. If social standing was involved, "Gentlemen's Agreements" could be relied upon to keep him in his place. If the curtain was drawn between natives and foreigners—well the Jew was usually a latecomer. Even when in our own times, he returned to his native soil of Palestine under a British mandate, he was classified as an immigrant. Every time an Iron Curtain was erected the Jew found his life more restricted, his existence more precarious.

To the everlasting glory of our people, however, we point

with justifiable pride to the striking historical fact that although the Jew always found Iron Curtains shutting him off from the world, he himself never sank to the level of his tormentors by becoming a builder of Iron Curtains himself. Quite the reverse. It has been the peculiar destiny of the Jew to be a builder of bridges, trying to bring men together, not to set them apart.

In a world where hatred for the stranger was universally accepted, he built the bridge of sympathy. "The stranger that sojourns with you shall be unto you as the native among you. And ye shall love him as yourself for ye were slaves in the land of Egypt."

In a world where each nation looked down with haughty pride and contempt upon others the Jew built the bridge of brotherhood. "Have we not all one Father, hath not one God created us all? Why then do we deal treacherously with one another?"

In a world where each religion believed itself to be in sole and exclusive possession of the key to salvation, the Jew built the bridge of tolerance. He who was the first to discover God taught that there were many highways to heaven. "The righteous among all peoples have a share in the world to come."

This contrast in the matter of religion received another striking documentation only a few weeks ago. The Jesuits meeting in Rome declared recently: "The Roman Catholic church, convinced through its divine prerogatives of being the only true church, must demand the right to freedom for herself alone."

Rabbi Judah Leib Fishman, the Israeli Orthodox Minister of Religions (note the plural-"religions"), speaking to the inhabitants of the conquered city of Nazareth, proclaimed full freedom for the practice of Christianity by the Christians. No further comment is necessary.

In a history full of strange ironies and puzzling paradoxes, not the least among them is the curious fact that while the world kept building Iron Curtains to shut him out, the Jew with stubborn persistence remained faithful to his consecrated role of being a builder of bridges between man and man. Edwin

Markham's poem, "Outwitted," seems to have been written especially for the Jew:

> "He drew a circle that shut me out
> Heretic, rebel, a thing to flout.
> But love and I had the wit to win
> We drew a circle that took him in."

If the Jew survived in spite of the Iron Curtains that were thrown up against him, it was because in addition to possessing the graciousness to build bridges for mankind he possessed the wisdom to build bridges for himself. As I see it, the significant bridges that the Jew erected for himself were three in number.

The first was the bridge between the Jew and God. That bridge we might call the Bridge of Prayer. The world at large has accepted the fact that the Jew was the first to formulate and teach the belief in the One Invisible God. But that supreme discovery, tremendous and revolutionary as it was, would have been of little practical value had it not been accompanied by another discovery—how to establish contact with the One God; how to reach God in moments of affliction when solace was needed, how to reach God in moments of bewilderment when vision was needed, how to reach Him in moments of despair when hope was needed, how to reach Him when a moral life preserver was needed to keep from drowning in the onrushing waters of immorality, perversity and inhumanity. The Jew's most significant contribution here was that he made God accessible through the Bridge of Prayer.

The pagans visualized their gods as inhabiting some distant eternal spheres remote from the cares and cries of their subjects. The Jews took God out of the heathen heavens and brought Him within reach of man. "In whatsoever place thou shalt mention my name, I shall come unto thee and bless thee." "The Lord is nigh unto all who call upon Him, to all who call upon Him in truth." To the question: "Where can God be found?" a chasidic rabbi answered in the true spirit of the faith, "Wherever He is admitted."

Thus, armed with, and strengthened by, this contact with his invisible ally, the Jew could be the victim of the world's madness and maintain his sanity; he could be humbled but never humiliated; he could be beaten but never defeated; he could be reduced to beggary and remain an aristocrat of the spirit. "The Lord is with me, I will not fear. What can man do unto me?"

Iron Curtains could block many an avenue of life but the Jew could always travel the highway to God on the Bridge of Prayer.

The second bridge the Jew built for himself was the bridge between himself and his tradition—that bridge we might call the Bridge of Education.

That the Jew is the creator of a powerful religious heritage is also a quite universally accepted truth, although I must hasten to add that the world doesn't know the half of it. The non-Jewish world only knows that the Jew wrote the Bible which it paid a rather doubtful compliment by calling it the Old Testament and regarding it merely as a prologue to the New. As far as the world knows, the genius of the Jew burned itself out in writing the Bible. The fact, of course, is that the Bible, far from being the last expression of the Jewish genius, is only the lofty preamble. After it, came that monument of five centuries of intense literary creativity—the Talmud. Then there was Jehuda Halevi, there was Saadia, there was Maimonides, there was Ibn Gabirol, there was Bialik and literally thousands of spiritual and literary giants.

But here again, the tradition, great as it was, was not the decisive thing. By itself, it was not enough. Greece also had a powerful legacy of philosophy, science, astronomy, art, mathematics. But, whereas, in Greece only the select few tasted of the fruits of the culture, among our people every Jew was an heir to the heritage. "The Torah which Moses commanded us is the inheritance of the whole congregation of Jacob." For the Jew had built for himself and his children the Bridge of Education.

Cecil Roth, the renowned historian, has vividly recorded the pervasiveness, the depth and the scope of learning which characterized the Jew throughout his history. "In an unlettered world, when even kings could not sign their names, they (the Jews) already had developed a system of universal education so that an illiterate Jew was, even in the Dark Ages, a contradiction in terms. Centuries before the modern idea of adult education was evolved, Jews regarded it as a religious duty to band themselves together for study every morning before the labors of the day began and every evening when the ghetto gates closed them off from association with the outside world." Mothers in their lullabies assured their children that "*Toire is die beste s'choirah*—Torah is the best of all worldly goods." Jewish mothers were always inspired by the example of the mother of Rabbi Joshua ben Chananyah who would take her child to the door of the academy in his crib so that his ears might become accustomed in infancy to the sound of learning.

Thus armed with a knowledge and a love of his tradition, the shafts of intolerance might torment the Jew's flesh, they could not wound his soul; they could threaten his position, they could not shake his pride; they could deprive him of his possessions, they could not loosen his grip on his spiritual patrimony. Would he change places with his oppressors? Every day he answered that question by saying: "*Ashraynu mah tov chelkenu*—Happy are we, how goodly is our heritage!"

Iron curtains could block many an avenue of life but the Jew could always travel the highway to his inheritance on the Bridge of Education.

The last bridge that the Jew built for himself was the bridge between himself and his people. That bridge we might call the Bridge of Fellowship.

Among no other people did there develop such an intense group loyalty and such a sturdy sense of community responsibility as there grew up among Jews. Superficially, one might say that outside pressure did that for the Jews. The hammer of prejudice pounded them into a solid mass. But anyone familiar with the inner rhythm of the Jewish group symphony must know that the Jew himself created his own instruments. In his prayers he rarely prayed for himself alone. Look through the prayerbook and see how few are the prayers written in the first person singular. The overwhelming majority are keyed to the "we" feeling. Even in the confessional of Yom Kippur, the Jew pleaded guilty to the sins of his fellow-Jew. "Al chet shechatanu—For the sins that we have sinned." When Jews, anywhere, were taken captive, Jews, everywhere, felt a personal obligation to provide ransom money.

In joy and in sorrow alike he depended upon his fellow Jews. If it was a wedding he wanted to celebrate, if it was a bris to be performed, if it was a kaddish that had to be recited, he needed at least nine other Jews. If it was kosher meat he wanted, if it was his children's education he was concerned with, he needed a Jewish community. For he, obviously, could not support a "Shochet" or a "Milamed" by himself. In every way the Jew wove the thread of his personal destiny into the community tapestry. Hillel's dictum: "Separate thyself not from the community," was the first "don't" on the social tablets of every Jew. For, as Prof. Mordecai Kaplan so aptly put it, the Jew could no more be a Jew by himself than one could be a soldier without an army. The greatest punishment the Jewish community could inflict upon one of its members was the Cherem, the ban of excommunication, forbidding anyone from having any contacts with him. Life for the Jew, cut off from the trunk of community living, became as impossible as it does for a branch severed from the life-giving tree. Attached to the community tree, he drew life-sustaining nourishment from the soil of the Jewish cooperative adventure.

Thus armed with a sense of belonging to his people the Jew could face exclusion and still feel at home; be confined to the ghetto and yet feel part of a mighty folk; be shut out from the world and know a deeper sense of comradeship than his jailers ever knew.

Iron Curtains could block many an avenue of life but the Jew could always travel the highway to his people on the Bridge of Fellowship.

The tragedy of the Jew today, my friends, is not so much that he still faces restrictive Iron Curtains from without. Our fathers found living as a Jew beautiful and worthwhile in the face of heavier and more numerous Iron Curtains. What makes the lot of the Jew particularly pathetic today is that he himself has largely blown up his Jewish bridges and has himself erected Iron Curtains in their stead.

Too many of us have blown up the Bridge of Prayer and shut ourselves in behind the Iron Curtain of secularism. A recent Gallup poll indicated that there are fewer Jews attending religious services proportionately than Catholics or Protestants. We, who taught the world how to pray, have largely forgotten the art ourselves. We, who gave the world the House of Prayer, frequent it least. We, who put together the immortal book of Psalms, the prayer-source of all Western religion, are least familiar with it. We who brought the world near to the one God, are furthest away from Him. We, who were once so intimate with God that we called Him, "Gottenyu, Tatenyu," are today hardly on speaking terms with Him. The Psalmist, in a moment of deep loneliness, cried out: "Ailee, Ailee, lamah azavtani?—My God, My God, why hast Thou forsaken me?" Sometimes as I look out upon the empty pews at services I wonder whether God isn't lonely too. I seem to hear Him cry out: "Ami, ami, lamah azavtani?—My people, my people, why have ye forsaken me?"

Too many of us have blown up the Bridge of Education and walled ourselves in behind the Iron Curtain of ignorance. As a group we are among the world's most literate, most cultured peoples. Jewishly speaking, however, our illiteracy has assumed alarming proportions. One of America's foremost writers of Jewish extraction, quotes the verse: "The stone which the builders rejected has become the chief cornerstone," and gives the source as Luke 20. If he knew his own people's Bible too, he would have known that Luke was merely quoting the 118th Chapter of Psalms. Today a Jew who only knows how to read Hebrew assumes in the eyes of his friends, and all too often in his own eyes, the stature of a Jewish scholar. Where our children are concerned, too many of us still envisage the function of Jewish Education as consisting exclusively of a basic training period for a Bar Mitzvah maneuver. We're not at all certain just what they are to get out of their Jewish education. The only thing of which we seem to be certain is that we don't want them to become rabbis—a fear, incidentally, which is as exaggerated as it is unwarranted. Of our Jewish heritage we might say, paraphrasing Churchill: "Never have so many known so little about so much."

Lastly, my friends, we have blown up the Bridge of Fellowship and shut ourselves in behind the Iron Curtain of isolation.

It is a sad commentary on the Jewish community spirit that in spite of everything that has happened in recent years to underscore the need of the Jew to work together with his fellow Jews, some 70% of American Jews have no Jewish affiliation whatsoever. They just don't belong at all. The Zionist organization last year, at the very pinnacle of its success, had less than 250,000 members or less than 5% of American Jewry. Coming a little closer to home, how many of us right here in the synagogue, honestly feel that what happens to the synagogue is of deep personal concern to us? There are, thank God, well over 1000 men and women in our synagogue tonight. How many of us can honestly feel that we have done our full share towards making this possible and are doing our share towards making possible the completion of the synagogue and the erection of a school building? How many of us, when approached for a building fund contribution, by self-sacrificing and over-worked men, answer their plea with resentment or, what is little better, give in a spirit of charity. A contribution to a synagogue building fund is not an act of charity. It is a supreme duty—an expression of an elemental sense of community responsibility. It is high time that more and more of us stopped leaning upon fewer and fewer of us so that with a reawakened sense of Jewish fellowship we might complete a task which is easily within the reach of all but is beyond the reach of a few.

If Judaism is to live, my friends, if our lives are to be the fruitful adventures they ought to be, there must be an end to Iron Curtains. We ourselves cannot destroy the Iron Curtains the world has thrown up against us. We can and must destroy the Iron Curtains that we ourselves have built.

On this Kol Nidre night let there be sounded the cry to batter the Iron Curtain of secularism, the Iron Curtain of ignorance and the Iron Curtain of isolation. Let there be an end to the barriers that keep us estranged from our God, from our tradition and from our people. Let us then go on to rebuild our bridges—the Bridge of Prayer, the Bridge of Jewish Education and the Bridge of Jewish Fellowship—so that we may once again come into living contact with our God, with our inheritance and with our people. Amen.